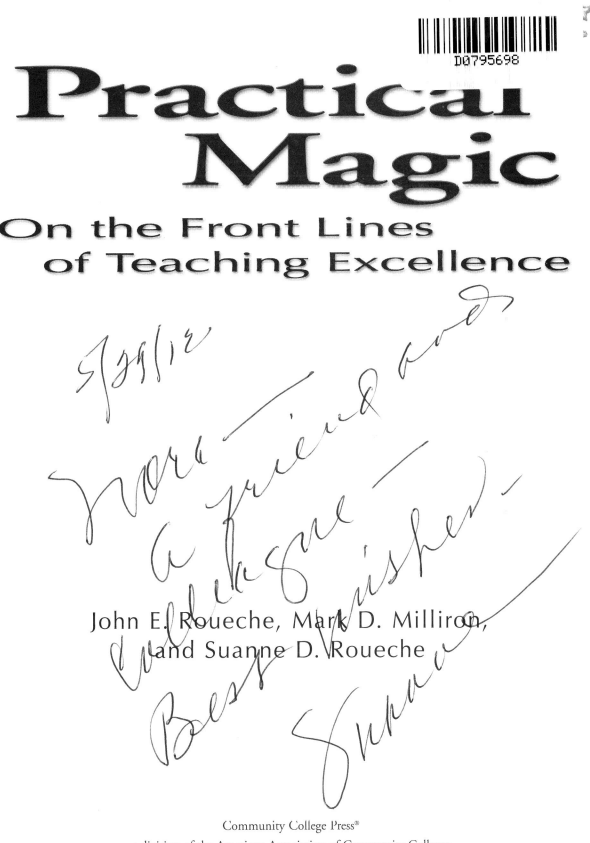

Practical Magic

On the Front Lines
of Teaching Excellence

John E. Roueche, Mark D. Milliron,
and Suanne D. Roueche

Community College Press®
a division of the American Association of Community Colleges
Washington, D.C.

The American Association of Community Colleges (AACC) is the primary advocacy organization for the nation's community colleges. The association represents 1,100 two-year, associate degree–granting institutions and more than 10 million students. AACC promotes community colleges through six strategic action areas: national and international recognition and advocacy, learning and accountability, leadership development, economic and workforce development, connectedness across AACC membership, and international and intercultural education. Information about AACC and community colleges may be found at www.aacc.nche.edu.

Design: Brian Gallagher Design
Editors: Jacqueline Edlund-Braun and Deanna D'Errico
Printer: Graphic Communications, Inc.

Community College Press
American Association of Community Colleges
One Dupont Circle, NW
Suite 410
Washington, DC 20036

Printed in the United States of America.

ISBN 0-87117-335-2

Contents

v   **Foreword**
     By George R. Boggs

vii   **Preface**

1   **Chapter One**
     On Recognizing Excellence: A Focus on the Best in the Room

15   **Chapter Two**
     A Study of the Architects of Teaching Excellence: NISOD
     Excellence Award Recipients

23   **Chapter Three**
     The Inspiration to Teach

35   **Chapter Four**
     Historical Overview of Teaching Excellence

59   **Chapter Five**
     Core Strategies for Effectively Teaching Content

79   **Chapter Six**
     Core Strategies for Effectively Teaching Students

95   **Chapter Seven**
     Assessing Learning: How We Know They Know

111   **Chapter Eight**
     Information Technology in Instruction

131   **Chapter Nine**
     Advice for Beginning Community College Instructors

147   **Chapter Ten**
     Implications and Recommendations for Planning and
     Practicing Teaching Excellence

161   **References**

173   **Appendix A: Five-Star Faculty Survey**

185   **Appendix B: Results of the Five-Star Faculty Survey**

193   **About the Authors**

195   **Index**

Foreword

We are living in a time of change, a time when the well-being and security of individuals and of society are more dependent than ever on educational levels and continued learning. Tomorrow's jobs will require higher skill levels and global and cultural understanding. Labor projections indicate that it will be a challenge for higher education to keep up with the demand for jobs that require higher-order skills. And given the significant demographic shifts in the population of the United States and other developed countries, our society will be challenged if we cannot find ways to educate all segments of our population, especially those who are now underserved by higher education.

Community colleges in the United States play a significant role in higher education. They are the colleges of choice for first-generation college students, for those who are underprepared for higher education, for minorities, and for students returning to education. More than 40 percent of all students in American higher education today are enrolled in community colleges. These institutions have changed the face of higher education in America by making it accessible and affordable. They are positioned to meet the educational needs of a changing society and thereby improve the quality of life for all people.

However, Roueche, Milliron, and Roueche set the context for *Practical Magic* with a discussion of the challenges facing community colleges themselves. A projected "tidal wave" of new students, increased competition from for-profit providers, decreasing levels of public funding, and increasing calls for accountability will test these institutions in unprecedented ways. If community colleges are to succeed in this increasingly difficult environment, they will have to remain true to their historical values of access, responsiveness, focus on student learning, and entrepreneurial action. They will need to focus on quality improvement and will need to document learning outcomes.

Community colleges are at the forefront of an educational reform movement that places student learning at the heart of the academic enterprise. In a "learning college," it is, indeed, everyone's job to promote and support student learning. Although everyone works to achieve and improve student learning, teachers are, of course, at the front line. The "learning college movement" has made the role of the teacher even more central to the college mission. As we learn more about how people learn, effective teaching has become much less focused on information transmission and more focused on creating the learning environment and on facilitation and inspiration. As Roueche, Milliron, and Roueche point out, the best teachers have always focused on students and their learning. The best teachers are, indeed, scholars of student learning. In *Practical Magic,* we learn what inspired those teachers, and we gain valuable insights into what makes them successful.

During my tenure as president of Palomar College in Southern California, I made it a point to interview the finalists for faculty positions. During the first year of teaching, I invited each new faculty member to have lunch or breakfast with me to talk about his or her experiences and to reinforce college values. Although these practices take a lot of time for a college president, there may be no better way for a leader to affect the quality of an institution than to actively participate in the employment and development of new faculty. There is no way that a college can be excellent if its faculty members are not.

In *Practical Magic,* Roueche, Milliron, and Roueche have made a significant contribution to what we know about teaching excellence, what motivates it, how learners are engaged, how teachers are using technology to improve student learning, and how learning is assessed. The book is a wonderful blend of theory, insights, and practical tips. It should be required reading for college leaders, new faculty, and directors of faculty development. With the important role that our colleges are being called on to play and with the challenges ahead, we will need more magicians on our campuses.

George R. Boggs
President and CEO
American Association of
Community Colleges

Preface

This report comes directly from the front lines of teaching excellence; it is intended to remind all of us in the teaching and learning enterprise that we are in a very complex business involving the intricate interplay among individuals, organizations, and diverse life situations. However, we focused solely on teachers and the perspectives they bring to their craft because we wanted to personalize the complexities with which this vital group grapples and provide some important grist for the current discussion, planning, implementation, and experimentation mills. Moreover, at a time when teaching as an art is often being disparaged, we intended to demonstrate clearly that the best of teachers have always been learning-centered innovators, bringing whatever tools and techniques they could muster to make a difference in student learning.

We aimed at being practical. Although we understand the importance of setting a useful context and we know that material from the fields of educational and cognitive psychology, from research data, and the like can be valuable additions to any discussion of teaching and learning, we wanted to focus primarily and extensively on how teachers help students learn, to share what we learned from exceptional teachers.

The stakes in education are high, and they compel us to reach for high performance. Colleges can accept nothing less than that in physical or virtual classrooms, specifically, and in the institution, generally. Given these demands, we went straight to the top to take advantage of the view and snap the most realistic and practical pictures of what is possible and most effective in teaching and learning today. In this case, we went directly to those at the top of their teaching fields, to those on the front lines whose talents in and out of the classroom and successes with their students have brought them recognition. They are the teachers we fondly describe as wielders of practical magic.

And so we sought to report on the perspectives, strategies, counsel, advice, and recommendations of thousands of teaching professionals who have received the National Institute for Staff and Organizational Development (NISOD) Excellence Award over the last decade. Recognized by their colleges for teaching excellence—and then by NISOD as their names are submitted for special recognition on NISOD's worldwide stage—these award recipients bring years of service and exemplary teaching and learning performance to this report. They share some of the best thinking available on the current teaching and learning scene.

Early on, we were joined by Cindy L. Miles, Vice President for Academic Affairs at Community College of Denver; Laurence F. Johnson, President and CEO of New Media Consortium; and Edward Leach, Vice President for Technology and Services at the League for Innovation in the Community College. They helped develop the protocol for the focus groups, were co-conveners and co-administrators of the first five focus groups, and participated in the development of the survey that was mailed to all award recipients. We are especially grateful for their guidance and expertise in the critical first steps of this study, and we felt their presence—their keen insights and good humor, in particular—as we completed other activities of this investigation and then finally prepared this report. Their contributions to this effort are much appreciated, and it is a far better document because of their talents and service.

Special thanks go out from us to Sheryl Powell, an executive assistant at NISOD, who once again—fortunate for us that history does repeat itself—brought her unique brand of excellence to this document, as she has done for at least six major reports of studies we have conducted over the last eight years. Her keen editing eye, her willingness to ride herd on the seemingly endless drafts and bibliography checks, and her ability to produce a final "clean" copy that "hangs together" just right, immeasurably improved all of our efforts.

The quality of the product indeed turns on and ultimately reflects the quality of the process. We knew that we would gather a rich mixture of great ideas and successful practices. But even we—with our collective histories of positive expectations—could not have anticipated being so overwhelmed by the breadth and depth of the *passion* that set the tone of the reward recipients' best individual and collective thinking.

It is that passion, in particular, that we hoped to capture in this book. If we failed at that, we have lost a glorious opportunity to describe and share the essence of the *power of practical magic* that makes this educational enterprise, the community college, a unique teaching and learning idea with such awesome potential for making great things happen.

However, we trust that the energy and wisdom in their words, ultimately, will carry the day. These excellent teachers whose ideas, strategies, and time-tested successes are making magic happen in undergraduate education collectively represent the best of what we are about in higher education and what we hope to be. It is for them we are grateful; it is to them that we dedicate this effort. It is their practical magic we applaud and celebrate!

Chapter One

On Recognizing Excellence:
A Focus on the Best in the Room

Striving for excellence in teaching is like running a race.... The prize is knowing you have made a difference in the life of a student. So I run the race of teaching, continually striving for that excellence that can make a difference.

—Judy Colwell, Northern Oklahoma College

When I was a beginner, I thought excellence meant knowing my subject. Twenty years and 240 sections of writing later, I know that excellence is initiating unawakened minds into the joys of thinking independently. My students don't always realize my part in that, but I do.

—Sue Tomlinson, Del Mar College (TX)

The history of community colleges is filled with mission and purpose statements, emphasizing both the centrality of teaching and the pursuit of excellence. No other institutions of higher education so emphasize learning as a priority, perhaps because community colleges' primary focus is on serving students and experiences—students who continue to come through their "open doors" in great numbers, seeking a viable pathway to a better life.

NISOD's Excellence Awards: A Tradition of Honoring the Best of the Best

Since 1978, the National Institute for Staff and Organizational Development (NISOD) has celebrated, supported, and encouraged teaching excellence with annual teaching and leadership conferences and weekly teaching tips publications (www.nisod.org/abstracts). It has recognized excellent teaching by college faculty, successful programs that make good on the promise that the open door implies, and effective instructional strategies that embrace and promote student success.

In 1989, after completing an intensive national study of teaching excellence in selected community colleges, NISOD faculty and staff celebrated the teachers who had participated as outstanding teaching professionals and were identified in the final report of findings and recommendations. As a heartfelt thank you to the more than 800 faculty so identified, NISOD held a commemorative ceremony in their honor during the final session of NISOD's annual conference in Austin, Texas; some of these faculty were in attendance at the conference. All 800 plus were declared recipients of the NISOD Teaching Excellence Award, identified in a special booklet that was distributed to all conference participants, and given a pewter medallion—similar to The University of Texas (UT) Teaching Excellence Award, modified for NISOD's use and approved by the UT System's Board of Regents. Either in person (if they were in attendance at the conference) or by mail, all recipients received this medallion, strung on a burnt-orange ribbon and suitable for displaying in their offices and wearing at college special events, including graduation.

The recognition ceremony was initially intended to be a one-time-only event. However, there was an unexpected outcome. NISOD faculty and staff simply had not anticipated the overwhelming response to this celebratory tribute to teaching excellence! Conference participants returned to their campuses, and NISOD began receiving inquiries from member colleges about how they might participate in future celebrations, how they might recognize some of their own excellent faculty.

Thus, a celebratory tradition began. Early each academic year, NISOD asks member-college presidents (more than 600 around the globe) to submit the names of individuals their colleges wish to recognize for teaching excellence. Selection criteria are left to the discretion of each institution. All individuals whose names are submitted are recognized as NISOD Excellence Award recipients. A special ceremony, held on the final day and session of the annual NISOD conference, features a video montage of Excellence Award recipients sharing their joys and philosophies of teaching and includes an opportunity for recipients to be physically "medallioned."

Few eyes witnessing this celebration each year are dry by the time deans, presidents, and colleagues from the colleges represented by these recognized faculty respectfully place medallions around the necks of their award recipients—individuals we have come to identify as "five-star" faculty. (All recipients are featured in the awards booklet and receive the pewter medallion that continues to provide a visual demonstration of appreciation and recognition. Recipients unable to attend the conference receive the medallion and booklet by mail.) More than 10,000 faculty members have been recognized over the life of this excellence awards program.

As we open each chapter that focuses on excellence award recipients' survey responses and focus group perspectives, we set the stage on which the recipients will be speaking. This stage does not demand an elaborate set, so we abbreviate the description of this context deliberately. We offer but a brief review of what has been learned from previous research, describe how this research links to practice, and provide some broadbrush descriptions of particulars of the state of the art. For example, we asked recipients about their most successful practices for teaching *content* and for teaching *students*. To set this stage, we created some typologies of learning principles and best practices in exemplary college teaching to consolidate some of the more useful background information into a bird's-eye view of major landmarks and hallmarks of what we know about good teaching.

Early on, we agreed that although it is always good research form to provide a rich, fully fleshed-out context to help develop an idea or support a thesis, we would seriously limit our stage settings to include only some of the most critical contextual issues. The purpose of this study was to capture the essence of practical magic described in the words of these award recipients. We wanted to focus squarely on the faculty themselves, closely examine what they shared with us, and write a useful guide that goes straight to the heart of the matter—the motivation, attributes, and characteristics of exemplary community college teachers. Our objective was to write a practical guide. As a result, readers will find that in some chapters we have simply let the participants' responses speak for themselves.

Setting the Stage: Challenges Posed by the Education Milieu

To appreciate more fully the roles and the performances of the actors on the stage, we must first fully appreciate the situations in which they live and work. If this study were an actual performance, the participants would be surrounded by complicated sets and fast-moving scenery changes, graphic depictions of these realities: major shifts in the purposes of education, growing diversity in student demographics and ways in which individuals attend college, increasing demands for improved institutional accountability, tight budgets and declining resources for services and programs, a seductive and dizzying array of options and applications of information technology, and increased competition among educational providers. The achievements and performances that earned these participants their awards appear even more extraordinary when we consider the milieu of change and challenge in which they were and are being accomplished.

Major Shifts in the Purposes of Education

"Education is necessary for the maintenance of a democracy.… Education is essential for the improvement of society.… Education helps to equalize opportunity for all people" (Roueche, 1968, pp. 7–8). These basic democratic philosophical assumptions supported the comprehensive educational system that fostered the development of community colleges. And, as community colleges began to embrace larger segments of the American population, the foundation of their growth was built on the convictions that higher education was the right of any individual who could profit from it and that colleges existed to serve the American people. Egalitarian notions clashed with meritocratic notions of access and opportunities. Community colleges have a remarkable history of description and delineation of the purposes they should and would serve in their communities; the pathways and journeys to the 21st century, especially those of access and performance, are well documented in the literature by critics and supporters alike. However, all in all, there is strong agreement that no one could have recognized or anticipated the burgeoning array of assignments these colleges would be handed—for better or worse, ready or not.

We need not dwell at any length on the enormous changes and developments in higher education over the last decade. Most likely, they are familiar by experience and educational literature, and certainly by widespread coverage in both local and national news reports. However, we point briefly to these major shifts in purpose—expectations and demands and options—as described in a recent report by the Association of American Colleges and Universities (AACU), *Greater Expectations: A New Vision for Learning as a Nation Goes to College* (2002). In their excellent discussion, the AACU national panel members observed that although Americans agree, generally, on their expectations for a college education, a diversity of interested parties hold widely divergent views about the purposes of college, specifically. Moreover, the panel members warned that these differences in views about purpose must be addressed if America is ever "to reap the potential benefits of expanded access" (AACU, 2002, p. 8). We draw directly from their good work to underscore the enormity of the problem and to capitalize on their ability to explain it succinctly, by organizing the discussion around the various interested parties.

Students. In the eyes of many students, whether traditional age or older adults, the college degree is the ticket to a good job. Some focus short term on their first appointment, and others on the longer-term promise of white-collar employment and at least a middle-class lifestyle. In choosing a college—largely by academic reputation—students expect job-related courses that will well prepare them to enter or change to their chosen careers and then advance within them (see Sax, Astin, Korn, & Mahoney, 2000).

Employers. Employers focus on the specific abilities they need in their employees. They expect colleges to graduate students able to perform consistently well, communicate effectively, think analytically, help solve problems, work collegially in diverse teams, and use relevant skills of the profession (see Business-Higher Education Forum, 1999). Increasingly, they expect technological and information literacy, and the private sector, in particular, looks for strong quantitative reasoning. Inconsistent results lead employers to question higher education's effectiveness and wish that its degrees, like technical certification, ensured documented levels of accomplishment.

Policymakers. Policymakers would like to see colleges and universities produce enough highly skilled graduates not only to satisfy workforce needs, but also to attract business and industry to local regions. They look for economic growth and improvements in statewide standards of living. As the demand for information- and technology-literate graduates (among others) is left unmet, higher education appears to be disengaged from many of these important societal needs.

Faculty. Ask college faculty members about the purpose of colleges, and most will explain their hope for students to engage intellectually and seriously with what is taught. Deep learning, they believe, develops the ability to defend positions based on knowledge, rather than simply on opinions. Professors expect students to write well and think clearly, explore multiple fields and modes of inquiry, and gain substantive knowledge in a particular field. As they see it, college learning should result in rational and reflective minds, open to continuous learning throughout a lifetime. The higher education community as a whole expects its members, both professors and students, to support free discussion that respects a variety of viewpoints and to embrace the active life of the mind.

The Public. Although the general public recognizes differences in prestige among colleges, it expects quality and empowering education from them all. Whether graduating from community or liberal arts colleges or from comprehensive or research universities, students are expected to be better at thinking and at knowledge-based work than after high school. The public anticipates that attendance will pay off in a more successful career, family life, and place in society. And although some important segments of society look for college graduates to assume leadership roles in the community, public attention focuses primarily on "getting into" to college, paying the bills, and then "getting out" with a degree. The public knows comparatively little about what actually happens during the college years (AACU, 2002, pp. 8–9).

These diverse views share many common purposes, and they can move toward a fundamentally more similar view of what being appropriately and reasonably well educated in America should and can mean, if we work toward a meeting of the minds regarding what America needs from the various members of an educated citizenry. Obviously, this nation can benefit from all of the purposes that these various stakeholders believe higher education can achieve and provide. However, what we can all agree on is that we are not living in the world in which our parents or, certainly, our grandparents lived.

Continuing Shifts in Student Demographics

Projections are that enrollment in colleges will continue to increase and that students will become more diverse as the numbers spiral up. Projections include the likelihood that by 2015, more than 2 million additional students will be enrolled, and many will be poor and minority students (Carnevale, 2000; Carnevale & Fry, 2001). The number of students over the age of 25 will continue to increase—14 percent by 2010 (National Center for Education Statistics [NCES], 2002b). More current data show that 28 percent of undergraduate students attend college part-time (Carnevale & Fry, 2001), and that number is much higher for community colleges: 73 percent of all undergraduates are nontraditional students (NCES, 2002a), 28 percent of all college students are minority students (NCES, 2002b), and more than half of all minority students enrolled in higher education are enrolled in community colleges.

Although 75 percent of high school graduates go on to continue some program of study (Education Trust-West, 2002), only 47 percent of them have completed what is regarded as a college prep curricula (Education Trust, 1999; Horn, Chen, & MPR Associates, 1998). And although almost half of all high school graduates complete a college preparatory curriculum (four years of English and three years each of math, science, and social studies;

Hartle & King, 1997), there is ample evidence that concerns about the quality of the instruction are justified. Almost half of all community college students are first-generation college attendees, and the majority is in need of financial assistance. In fact, in 1999, 74 percent of full-time students worked while attending school—46 percent at least 25 hours per week and 20 percent at least 35 (King & Bannon, 2002). More than 60 percent of students working at least 25 hours per week indicate that they would not be able to attend college were it not for their part-time employment, and large numbers admit that their work hours create problems with their grades, their school schedules, and their choice of courses (King & Bannon, 2002).

Moreover, approximately half of all first-time students matriculating at community colleges test as academically deficient in at least one basic skills area (McCabe & Day 1998; Milliron & Leach, 1997; Smith, Young, Bae, Chayand, & Alsalam, 1997)—typically, that single category is mathematics (NCES, 1996). The U.S. population is becoming more diverse; historically, data link minority groups to educational underpreparedness, with strong links to inadequate facilities in their schools and their communities; and the gaps between high- and low-income levels and college completion have not changed (Hartle & King, 1997). The news that poverty rates in the United States are "among the highest in the developed world" is overwhelming (Hodgkinson, 1997, p. 7). And, finally, the immigrant population is expanding, up by more than 50 percent in the last decade (Hodgkinson, 1997); the large majority are unprepared for work in today's skilled workforce.

Clearly, there are a significant number of characteristics that put students at risk. The majority of students enrolling in community college credit programs are characterized by the following challenges to successful academic performance:

- first-generation learners with little support
- pathways to success unknown
- poor self-image
- never left the neighborhood
- failure, self-defeatism, or unreachable goals
- work 30 hours per week and subject to social ills
- average age 29
- returning women
- large minority student population
- increasing numbers of foreign-born students
- economic insecurity: one-third below poverty level
- desperation, economically driven
- academically weak
- in the top 99 percent of high school graduating class
- poor or low test scores or GED scores (data are from Roueche & Roueche, 1993, p. 39)

This list has changed little over the last 30 years; it identifies an overwhelming number and variety of academic, social, and economic circumstances that students bring with them to college. Economic realities, bleak futures, and low-paying jobs drive students to seek training and pursue other educational experiences. An unconscionable number arrive woefully unprepared and underprepared for the rigors, challenges, and requirements of college-level work.

Increasing Demands for Improved Institutional Accountability

According to Astin (1985), "[T]rue excellence lies in the institution's ability to affect its students and faculty favorably, to enhance their intellectual and scholarly development, and to make a positive difference in their lives" (1985, pp. 60–61). Tightening institutional effectiveness measures, commonly accepted value-added approaches to measuring quality, and the like are becoming standard operating procedures as the public—stakeholders inside and outside the institution—becomes increasingly critical of colleges' performance and products.

The Community College Roundtable (1994) identified 13 core indicators that, although not totally comprehensive, appear to reflect the most critical functions typically addressed in community college mission statements:

- student goal attainment
- persistence (fall to fall)
- degree completion rates
- placement rate in the workforce
- employer assessment of students
- number and rate who transfer
- performance after transfer
- success in subsequent related course work
- demonstration of citizenship skills
- client assessment of programs and services
- responsiveness to community needs
- participation rate in service area (pp. 16–25)

Although no one can argue with the significance of each of these indicators to measuring institutional effectiveness, no one can deny the current enormous challenges—for example, increasing student diversity and reduced funding—to colleges' achieving high marks for their performance.

But achieve them they must: Increasing numbers of states are now directly linking performance measures to the funds they budget for higher education. Currently, nearly one-half of all states require institutions to conduct some student learning assessments (Roueche, Johnson, & Roueche, 1997). Moreover, many state legislatures openly discuss the realities that higher education could well become a discretionary item on their budgeting agenda. Ignoring accountability challenges or poor performing will only attract harsher penalties for underachievement —that is, financial support will ebb away from noncompliant and low-performing institutions. Funding is ever more typically tied to accountability. As researchers such as Roueche et al. (1997) have warned:

> Colleges can seriously attend to the wake-up call being made by accrediting agencies, legislators, and the public—and respond in sincere, timely, and positive ways—or they can look forward to more stringent and more intrusive measures than currently exist. They must either embrace the effectiveness tiger or be eaten by it. (p. vii).

Suggestions for how best to accomplish this abound, but the more common overarching recommendation is that colleges can, and should, establish clear benchmarks for achievement, students' work should be examined against those benchmarks, and external examiners should be involved in the assessment process (Ward, 2001). Having goals and standards for student learning, most appropriate in a postsecondary context, is an important nut to crack in crafting accountability models and implementing them (Wellman, 2001).

Tighter Budgets and Declining Resources for Services and Programs

Research data warn that funding from traditional sources will continue to decline. In a June 2002 survey by the State Higher Education Executive Officers' Organization, results indicated that only 23 states had final budget information available, 39 percent of these 23 had cuts in their postsecondary budgets, and another 30 percent had less than a 1 percent increase in their appropriations (Johnstone & Poulin, 2002).

Cutbacks in state spending and other reductions in state support, as well as reductions in support from other traditional sources, have prompted colleges to look for ways to bring in additional dollars. Many colleges are choosing, with regret, to increase tuition and fees. Recent reports indicate that tuition increases rose faster than the projected rate of inflation in 35 of 50 states in 2001–2002 (*Chronicle of Higher Education*, 2002). The increased financial burdens on college students are obvious, and they promote potential dead ends for students already living in marginal economic circumstances.

Enrollment trend watchers tell us that all reports indicate that student enrollment is climbing in U.S. community colleges; total college enrollments are projected to be 16 million by 2004, up from fewer than 15 million in 2000 (*Chronicle of Higher Education*, 2002). Increasing demands for services against a backdrop of decreasing funding can stimulate creative thinking, at colleges' best. Responses to bleak funding news are mixed, but many colleges are investigating and implementing strategies by which they can improve their fund-raising performance, or "friend raising" (Chapman, 2001), sponsoring multiple opportunities by which their communities can discover new benefits that their college provides or savor those with which they are familiar. Many colleges are encouraging faculty to become more involved in revenue and constituency development, including grant writing, becoming more involved in service to the community, and identifying entities with whom the college could partner to provide support for current and developing programs, student scholarships, and the like (Roueche, Roueche, & Johnson, 2002).

An Increasing Array of Information Technology Applications

E-learning, or technology-enabled learning, is causing a major stir in every camp that has a stake or other interest in the seductive possibilities that information technology (IT) describes and offers to the most savvy and those far less experienced (Milliron & Miles, 2001). Arguments abound about how deep and wide community college investments should be, including: they should stick to their knitting—do what they have always done best and what they can best afford; community colleges should not consider competing against for-profit competitors who have far greater access to capital markets that can finance the technology infrastructures they must provide or strengthen in order to increase their appeal to relatively untapped, enormous markets (especially in foreign, less-developed countries; Cappelli, cited in Pittinsky, 2002). As funding levels continue to decline and demand for new and improved services continues to increase, critics of the rush to e-learning argue that community colleges can ill afford to experiment with strategies or initiatives "in the name of unproven benefits" (Pedersen, 2002, p. 18).

Proponents of e-learning urge colleges to consider carefully "how it will improve…services…products, and…bottom line" (Coné, 2001, p. 1). When asking college constituents why they are thinking about getting involved with information technology, at any level and to any degree, e-learning designers hear these typical responses: "Apparently, the train is leaving, and I'd better be on it…we want to reduce costs or avoid increased costs…we just want to be more effective" (Coné, 2001, p. 1). When Coné, former vice president of Dell Learning (at Dell Computer, Inc.), recently addressed a large audience of college presidents, he made these recommendations for helping smooth and inform the transitions their institutions make to technology-enabled learning:

- Know where you are going and why.
- Be sure that you are ready.
- Know that it may require changes in practice and in philosophy.
- Realize that you can't hide from the world. (Coné, 2001, p. 4)

Current discussions about IT are rarely about whether to apply it to business, instruction, and the like, but rather how deep and wide the applications should, can, and will be. Common questions include the following: How much do we know about what we need, how do we find out what we do not know, how do we finance what we want and need, and how do we gear up to use the technology most effectively and efficiently? Moreover, there are deeper purposes to emerging dialogues on IT. Millions of students in the United States are "digitally disenfranchised," watching this e-world pass them by bit by bit. They are unable to access economic and personal opportunities because of lack of access to and instruction in IT (de los Santos, de los Santos, & Milliron, 2000).

Discussions about this growing digital divide lead to calls for education to engage e-learning strategies to help "bridge the divide." However, some argue that it is time to raise the stakes even higher and move beyond discussions about the digital divide imperative for education to dialogues about "education in a digital democracy." In a deeply connected, technology-driven world, the ability of our students to live free may hang in the balance, as business, political, religious, hate groups, and terror organizations scramble to use e-technologies to manipulate and take advantage of the least educated and most vulnerable of citizens (Milliron & Johnson, 2002; Milliron & Miles, 2001). From this perspective, the call is to help students learn not only about or with technology, but also about how not to be used by it.

What we know is that the responses to these questions are all about and will require change, and, in any venue, change faces resistance. In 1513 Machiavelli said "It must be considered that there is nothing more difficult to carry out, nor more doubtful to success, nor more dangerous to handle, than to initiate a new order of things." Colleges report that in addition to resistance to change itself, other issues—such as training and access—muddy the institutional waters and create conversion, application, and implementation problems, collectively putting them, as one college reported, on the "bleeding edge" of technological transformation. "Something that may begin as a single, insignificant change may become a revolution" (Halttunen, 2002, p. 28).

Researchers of change strategies encourage (1) education plus communication—once people are persuaded, they will often help with the implementation of the change; however, the more people involved, the more time-consuming the process becomes; (2) participation plus involvement—people who participate will be committed to implementing change; (3) manipulation plus co-optation—a relatively quick and inexpensive solution to resistance problems, but it can lead to future problems if people feel manipulated; and (4) explicit plus implicit coercion—speedy and can overcome resistance but can be risky if it leaves people angry with the initiators (Kotter, 1995).

Colleges grappling with the complexities and the ambiguities associated with information technology—from the micro (classroom) to the macro (institutionwide) applications—report that as discombobulating as these issues are, they fuel important discussions about current challenges of internal demands and external competition. Ultimately, colleges must ask themselves: Can we reasonably embrace the technology? What can we do better than other providers—that is, why would students prefer our colleges over any other entity or provider? What is our role in enabling the digitally disenfranchised? What is our role in helping students live free in a digital democracy?

Increased Competition Among Education Providers

In addition to the more than 2,300 private colleges competing for higher education market shares (*Chronicle of Higher Education*, 2002), growing numbers of for-profit challengers are even more serious competitors for community college students. Some of the most familiar for-profit educational providers are the University of Phoenix (with 58 campuses and 102 learning centers in 36 states, Puerto Rico, and Vancouver, British Columbia; 25,000 students from 50 states and 47 foreign countries enrolled in its online campus; and articulation agreements with 150 community colleges); DeVry Institutes (with 21 campuses in the United States and Canada and more than 47,000 full- and part-time students); Great Britain's Open University, with more than 200,000 students; and ITT Technical Institute (with 70 institutes in 28 states, 25,000 students, and arguably awarding the most electronics and drafting degrees of any provider; Roueche et al., 2002).

The primary marketplace challenges to community colleges come with the for-profits emphasis on career-oriented, hands-on, and customer-focused programs appealing to new types of students. Working adults and parents with families are drawn to their offerings of accelerated programs, flexible schedules, and convenient locations. The individualized attention and support they provide are particularly attractive to nontraditional students. And, workforce demands that graduates demonstrate specific competencies that employers require have helped drive the development and growth of the vendor-based certificate market. Data indicate that by early 2000, more than 2.4 million information technology certificates had been awarded and more than 300 vendor-provided certificates are available currently (Elsner, 2001).

Other challenges are obvious in the for-profits' abilities to "cherry pick" the most profitable programs, leaving public community colleges to provide higher-cost, lower-demand programs. The for-profits are active politically; they build strong political relationships that, in some states, now limit the ability of community colleges to advertise. On the national scene, the Career College Association—the national association of for-profit career colleges (www.career.org)—resigned its association with and place on the Board of the American Council on Education, specifically to free itself to lobby for the specific interest of career colleges as the reauthorization of the Higher Education Act comes before Congress. And, as it lobbies, this group is quick to note that its success is measured by high rates of student retention, degree completion, job placement, and employer satisfaction—leading some to argue that it may be more sensitive to quality concerns than are the more traditional community colleges.

Over the past decade, there has been a 78 percent increase in the number of two-year institutions and a 266 percent increase in four-year institutions. Enrollment in the for-profits has grown by 59 percent, to roughly 365,000 students. Nationwide, the for-profit share of the two-year college market grew from 19 to 26 percent.

Although arguments will continue in the foreseeable future, it is clear that no educational institution would choose to turn its back totally on the fallout and possibilities of the IT explosion. Community colleges are going forward with implementation and applications, albeit at varying speeds, breadth, and depth. The for-fee, for-profit competitors in the educational market are increasing their efforts for larger market shares, and they have an enticing array of advantages that tilt the scales their way. There are strong arguments, however, coming from outside college walls, especially from technology vendors, who are drawing from their perspectives of community colleges' traditions and strengths to counter the views that for-profits have the inside track to this lucrative market. They (e.g., Tarence, 2002) contend that community colleges

- are poised to profit because of several comparative advantages, including credibility as proven educators and strong corporate and community relationships
- are able to organize and choreograph the distribution of training, content, instructional technology, and services around the needs of the educational consumer
- are especially positioned to mediate educational services transactions between producers and consumers, creating value for both parties
- are poised to develop a fertile context for learning and training that is best-of-breed and defensible in the market by adding value to the learning transaction
- can bond the customers to their brand and keep them coming back for all lifelong learning needs
- have the ability to combine learning technology with content and then wrap high value around this content through creative packaging and presentation

Conclusion

The array of challenges in the various props and actions that we have depicted in today's educational milieu should promote community colleges' best thinking about what it will take to be the best in teaching and learning. These extraordinary pressures require colleges to develop fundamentally different views and ways of doing whatever it takes to survive and, ultimately, prosper in these turbulent times. Pressures of turbulence and change also require responses from individuals who collectively and individually agree that they have a responsibility to students, their communities, and themselves to strive toward becoming the best they can be. We propose that colleges who staff themselves with individuals who encourage, support, and provide excellent teaching will not be disappointed in their own performance when the votes are counted. It is the work of talented, engaged, and practical individuals upon which community colleges' best traditions are built; it is they who provide the special energy these unique teaching and learning institutions require to "carry out…their mission with spirit and élan" (Smith, 1990, p. 19). We turn now to describing this study, in which we listened carefully to the individuals who are the heart of the institution and the keys to its success—community college teachers on the front lines of teaching excellence.

Chapter Two

A Study of the Architects of Teaching Excellence: NISOD Excellence Award Recipients

*Words don't operate in a single realm
but have a life outside the page.*

—Starbuck (2002)

Wset out to study more than a decade of NISOD's Excellence Award recipients—these architects of teaching excellence—by focusing on their words and wisdom, insights and practices. Our primary interest was to explore what makes these extraordinary women and men successful and to inform the academy about the best in teaching and learning as seen through the eyes and from the experiences of seasoned and celebrated professionals.

To accomplish this task, we knew that our performance in reporting and describing must do justice to their words and retain the energy with which they were shared with us. More than once, we were charged by study participants with being the best we could be as we nurtured this project, ensuring that their words would literally jump off the page and take root in the fertile ground of community colleges everywhere. This challenging charge stays with us to this day.

Tradition and innovation color the hybrid fabric of this research and continue the commitment to honoring community college teaching excellence from which the NISOD celebration arose. As previously noted, the first cohort of 869 Excellence Award recipients was honored in May 1989 for their participation in a national study of teaching excellence conducted by The University of Texas (Baker, Roueche, & Gillett-Karam, 1990). In addition, this investigation follows and extends the research tradition established by Peters and Waterman (1982) of profiling excellence in American business by identifying the attributes and actions of exemplary models. This approach has been applied in the field of education, first to the study of excellence in America's public schools (Roueche & Baker, 1986) and subsequently to profiles of excellence in community colleges (Baker et al., 1990; Roueche & Baker, 1987; Roueche, Baker, & Rose, 1989). From these studies arose profiles of successful businesses, schools, and colleges, as well as of effective leaders within these organizations—composites of exemplars that exceed the characteristics and behaviors of any one subject of study but which represent ideals by which others may chart a course toward excellence.

Innovation is woven into the study's design and generative implications. We intended to do more with this study than dissect effective undergraduate teaching, identify its salient features, and offer up another listing, however valid, of good practices that faculty can adopt to transform themselves into "superteachers." Believing that exemplary teachers are greater than the rational sum of their parts, we share Brookfield's (1990, p. 192) concern about researchers who decontextualize the "inchoate messiness of college teaching" in attempts to define simple rules of practices to be followed as standards for effectiveness.

We all live in a world of relationships and change that makes prediction and uniformity impossible (Wheatley, 1994). With that reality in mind, we decided to counter traditional reductionist research methods with new interactive qualitative methods involving study subjects—community college faculty and students—not only in data generation but also in data analysis activities. The profiles of teaching excellence offered by this research resemble what Sternberg and Horvath (1995, p. 9) called prototypes—clusters of theoretically grounded, yet empirically based, families of features shared by exemplars that represent the central tendency of those identified as excelling in the subject under study.

Prototypes provide a basis for understanding common factors or practices of exemplars yet allow for diversity in the population and assume there is no exact model that all cxcmplars meet (Sternberg & Horvath, 1995). We believe the prototype view of exemplary practice in community college teaching, offered by this study, not only contributes to our understanding of community colleges' teaching effectiveness but also provides rich fodder for the continuing dialogue about the changing roles of college faculty.

Several factors make this study timely. Since the first cohort of Excellence Award recipients were honored in 1989, the number of two-year colleges formally recognizing and rewarding exemplary faculty has grown. Andrews (1995) reported that the proportion of two-year colleges with merit recognition programs for faculty increased from 20 percent in 1985 to 60 percent in 1991. In a 1995 national survey, Jenrette and Hays (1996) found programs to recognize exemplary teaching in almost 70 percent of responding two-year institutions. Although one of NISOD's primary interests, initially, was to encourage colleges to recognize teaching excellence as a component of their own faculty and professional development programs and activities, it cannot rightly take too much credit for this increase in merit recognition efforts. The times for supporting exemplary behaviors aimed at improving retention rates and increasing student successes were upon us in the last decade of the 20th century, as stakeholders in higher education were asking ever more serious questions about institutional performance and effectiveness.

We argue that colleges were beginning to take considerably more interest in identifying and rewarding the faculty who were keys to improving services and outcomes. Whatever the reasons, the fact that such increases in recognition occurred is justifiably impressive. However, despite such increased attention to recognizing teaching effectiveness, the literature reveals no comprehensive investigation of exemplary community college teaching since 1990. Hence, we had even more reason to conduct this present study.

Overview of the Study

As was described in chapter 1, this is a time of great social change and redefinition of the role of institutions of higher education in preparing future generations of global citizens. As the most economically efficient and accessible segment of higher education, community colleges have become the institutions of choice for more than half of this nation's college students and the leading point of entry to higher education for people of color, low-income students, and immigrants to this country (Boone, 1997; Koltai, 1993). As the new millennium dawned, greater demands were being made on community colleges and their faculties to serve growing numbers of underprepared college students. In the current climate of rapid workforce change, community colleges are especially needed to provide quality postsecondary education, new job skills training, and retraining of workers whose jobs have been lost. Community college faculty have been recognized for a remarkable period of time as the most adaptive and committed teachers in higher education. This study pays tribute to and explores the success factors of these faculty from the institutions that Page Smith (1990, pp. 19–20), noted historian and author of *Killing the Spirit: Higher Education in America*, called the "hope" of American higher education.

We intended to cast this book in a context and format that could best provide a holistic portrait of the philosophy, motivation, attributes, and practices of successful community college faculty. The very comprehensive set of seven research questions were drawn from six original, more general questions that addressed some of what we believed to be the most critical issues in preparing future teachers and capturing the best current teaching and learning practices. Essentially, we wanted to know the following:

- What inspired successful faculty members to pursue teaching as a career?
- What techniques and practices do they rely on in their classrooms to promote learning?
- How do they connect with and motivate increasingly diverse groups of students with a dizzying array of educational goals and needs?
- How do they relate to the explosion of information technology that is transforming educational needs worldwide?
- What advice do they have for beginning community college instructors?
- How do they know when their efforts are successful and learning is taking place?

Overall, our inquiry was grounded in a conceptual context of existing theories of learning and findings from more than 70 years of research on effective college teaching.

The remainder of this book focuses on the rich findings drawn from faculty recognized for their exemplary performance; however, for those readers who are interested in the study design and procedures, we provide a brief overview of our methods. We conducted the study in a two-stage format, blending interactive qualitative techniques and standard quantitative survey methodologies. We were intrigued with the "hybrid vigor" (Miles & Huberman, 1994, p. 310) that this mixture is purported to exhibit; it is what attracted us to this format and what essentially gave us the results that would be most useful and valuable for members of learning communities anywhere.

We called on the strengths of each methodological approach, first using an interactive qualitative method to explore faculty perspectives along a number of instructional lines—focus groups of award recipients who were attending the 1997 NISOD conference and were invited to join peers and colleagues in these special two-hour conference sessions. Then we turned to quantitative survey methods (1) to test the agreement with the findings from these focus groups within the larger population of award recipients and (2) to construct a priority ranking of faculty views on the issues identified in the first study stage. This triangulation of methods and sources increased both the quality and the rigor of the analysis. To further explain the process, we include the details of the study's two stages.

Stage One: Interactive Qualitative Focus Groups

Five two-hour focus group sessions were held during the May 1997 NISOD International Conference on Teaching and Leadership Excellence. All award recipients were invited to attend, but groups were limited to 50 participants each. A total of 230 participants attended the sessions. The average age of the participants was 50; approximately 53 percent were male and 47 percent female.

In each focus group, faculty were asked to participate in a process of collaborative brainstorming and idea-clustering activities, known in total quality management circles as *affinity diagramming*—a group process for organizing large amounts of language or textual information, originally designed for strategic organizational management and planning (Brassard, 1989). However, in this study, it was used as an interactive group data collection and analysis process. The faculty members were asked to respond to research questions, then participate in group analysis of these responses—ultimately grounding the study's findings in their collective experiences while offering participants opportunities to share individual perspectives.

Seven questions, drawn from the original six more general research questions, became the focus of the study, being identified as the most targeted and useful questions we could address in this investigation. The questions were posted around the walls of a large conference room; ample space was provided around each question to allow participants to post their responses. The research questions, targeted at the heart of the matter, were as follows:

1. What inspired you to become a teacher?
2. What are the core strategies you use to be an effective teacher of content?
3. What strategies do you use to be an effective teacher of students?
4. How do you know learning is going on?
5. In what ways do you use information technology in instruction?
6. What do you see as the key issues (positives or problems) in the use of technology in instruction?
7. What advice would you give a beginning community college instructor?

We reviewed the questions with each group and then asked participants to post their responses nearest the question being answered (using Post-it® notes and including only one answer on each note). To a background of soft, soothing music, the participants moved around the room, posting their "notes" alongside and all around the questions, a process that took approximately 45 minutes. Participants were absorbed in their work during that process—animated discussions bubbled up between and among these teaching colleagues, and deliberate, purposeful progress was made from question to question as they completed their posting tasks.

When the posting process wound down, we divided the group into seven small groups, and each group was assigned one of the seven questions and asked to arrange the posted responses to that particular question into thematic clusters (affinity groups). That process took approximately 45 minutes, and then each group reported on its findings. Finally, we began a discussion in which individual faculty members could explain their responses in greater depth than the size of the Post-it® notes would allow. This discussion was videotaped for secondary analysis purposes. After all focus group sessions had been held and the conference concluded, a research team led by the authors reviewed the affinity groups for each question and created a master set of thematic clusters.

Stage Two: Quantitative Survey Method

We designed a questionnaire (see Appendix A, "Five-Star Faculty Survey"), listing the research questions and the thematic clusters (expressed as statements, with an example comment for each) that had been generated by the faculty in stage one. Respondents were asked to record their level of agreement with each statement by choosing one item from a variation of a standard 7-point Likert scale:

YES! Yes yes ? no No NO!

In addition, respondents were asked to rank their responses by identifying the top three statements with which they most agreed.

We mailed the questionnaire to the entire population of award recipients—a total of 6,958—recognized from the beginning of this rich tradition to 1997, the year in which we held the first focus group sessions. We made several follow-up efforts to locate faculty who had moved since receiving their awards or had retired and whose surveys were returned as undeliverable.

A total of 1,670 faculty responded (24 percent), which is a high percentage given the likely turnover in this cohort over time. The returned surveys were coded into an SPSS statistical package and the results tabulated for the demographic, modified 7-point Likert scale, and ranking questions. The Likert-scale data were reported in a simple frequency distribution table along with each item's mean score. The ranking responses were reverse coded to give 3 points to an item assigned a rank of 1 by the respondents, two points to a rank of 2, and one point to a rank of 3. The final rankings were calculated based on which items were assigned the highest number of total points. Each question's item responses were then ordered based on rank and listed along with Likert frequency percentages and means.

The demographics of the survey respondents were amazingly similar to those of the first five focus groups—the average age was 50, 56 percent were male and 44 percent female, community college teaching experience averaged 17 years, and almost one in four planned to retire within five years. As will be more fully discussed in the chapters that follow, the Likert frequency data coupled with the ranking data validated the work of the focus groups and further fleshed out the faculty perspectives voiced in the previous discussions. Although there clearly are differences in preferences for the responses, we believe this two-stage qualitative and quantitative process captured well the key strategies, suggestions, and issues identified by faculty members.

So, by 1998–1999, almost 2,000 award recipients from around the world had shared their perspectives with the research team. Sifting through and organizing our findings began in earnest in 2000–2001; simultaneously, we conducted individual interviews with randomly selected faculty from a sizable group of participants who had indicated an interest in additional discussion with a member of the research team. We continued to update significant supporting and clarifying information and data that we agreed should be included in our presentation of the responses to individual research questions and related discussions.

Then, as we entered the final stages of our study, we elected to host yet another round of focus group sessions in 2002 at the NISOD conference, inviting current Excellence Award recipients to participate in a less formal and more unstructured format than we used in 1997, but one in which the most recent cohort of recipients could share their perspectives on the seven research questions and play off each other's responses. More than 60 participants were involved in each of the two one-hour sessions. Each participant received a copy of the tabulated, most typical comments taken from the survey responses to the research questions, as submitted by the 1,670 recipients. Each was also given an abbreviated survey that included the seven research questions and questions that would provide demographic data about the participants in these final focus sessions.

Before we began the large-group discussions, we announced that we preferred that they limit their responses to answering only two research questions, given the limited time available. We were especially interested in hearing their responses to questions #4 and #7: "How do you know learning is going on?" and "What advice would you give a beginning community college instructor?" In particular, we were looking to gather additional responses to question #4: As we had discovered in the literature, particularly in studies related to measurement and evaluation, and in diverse assessments of learning, this area was surprisingly and regrettably teaching's weakest link. So we continued to gather strategies and insights from the professionals who were on the front lines in responding to the most serious teaching and learning challenges.

Before opening the floor to discussion, we asked that participants look at the materials we had provided and to restrict their responses to new information or clearly unique perspectives. For the most part, the participants followed that directive, although many took the opportunity to underscore or expand upon a particular perspective already included in the tabular documents. A number of these focus group participants responded to our invitation to be interviewed at some later date and prior to completing this report. The majority of these final focus group participants submitted written responses to the abbreviated survey prior to leaving the session. Others submitted their responses after the conference. Again, the demographics of these most recent participants were strikingly similar to those of the first five groups, as well as to the survey respondents.

We summarized the qualitative and quantitative responses to the survey questions in tables (see Appendix B, "Results of the Five-Star Faculty Survey"). Each table highlights a survey question and the thematic cluster of responses derived from the focus groups when that question was addressed. An example comment that captures the essence of the shared perspectives in that cluster is included on the right-hand side of the table. To the left of each category and comment, we provide the Likert-scale responses from the national survey and the mean response for each comment. To the far right on each table, we provide the weighted ranking of the survey responses. Focus group responses are listed in order of overall priority ranking of survey responses.

As we brought to a close this investigation of more than 2,000 NISOD Excellence Award recipients, our hearts and our minds had been captured by these professionals—their commitment to the art of teaching and their advocacy of eminently practical strategies for touching lives. We could almost feel the magic of their work in teaching and reaching students. In short, we were looking at extraordinary pictures of what is possible in the improvement of college teaching and learning. The task before us, then, was honoring this artistry— capturing these vivid hues, extraordinary images, and striking compositions in an authentic and useful portrait of their practical magic. We turn now to the results of that effort.

Chapter Three

The Inspiration to Teach

Our aspirations are our possibilities.

—Samuel Johnson

Undoubtedly, we become what we envisage.

—Claude M. Bristol

Of all the chapters, this was by far the most interesting and exciting to write. Strangely, we did not follow our usual order of things, our pattern of beginning at the beginning. In this case, the logical beginning would have been with what inspired these award recipients to become teachers, but we were never able to stay focused on that beginning. Instead, we attended to the particulars of the other research questions. Looking back on this organizational protocol, we agreed that, doubtlessly, we were working from our own modified version of the French admonition: "In order to teach Johnny, you must first know Johnny." In order to get our arms around the full significance and capture the passion of the responses, we had to really know these award recipients.

We agreed that we achieved that, primarily, by reliving the focus group discussions through our voluminous notes and documents and through the survey responses and analyzing the data and comments. Then, armed with the knowledge base we needed to address their passion and energy, we could just enjoy immensely the self-reports of inspiration. We did, and we trust that all teachers and all of us who have been well taught will see some of themselves and their experiences jumping off the pages of this chapter.

This is one of the chapters in which we were not compelled or even tempted to construct context or expand on the messages and perspectives that were shared. These chapters include thoughts so personal and so unique to the individuals who participated in this study that we just stood back and let their words carry the day. We offer only the "bookends" for their contributions.

We open with a true story. Several years ago, just a few months before the annual NISOD conference in May, the NISOD director received a letter written by an Excellence Award recipient. Because recipients are encouraged to submit a thumbnail sketch of their educational philosophies (and many were submitted in letters to the director), the letter landed in the "in" box and was opened along with so many others that were full of excitement and expectations for the future. However, this letter stopped us in our tracks. In brief, this award recipient told us that his doctor had advised him to get his affairs in order in due haste and that, because his condition was worsening, in all likelihood he would not be alive to receive the award in person at the NISOD conference. However, he wanted to share with us how delighted he was to have received such recognition for work he felt privileged to do. Furthermore, he wrote: "Two things I know for sure at this time in my life: I would marry the same woman again, and I WOULD BE A TEACHER!" For years thereafter, this letter was read during the awards celebration at the close of the NISOD conference. He had no idea how many hearts and minds would be touched by his words; they inspired us all to be at our best. We wished we had had the opportunity to ask him, as we did the participants in this study: "What inspired you to become a teacher?"

Responses to "What Inspired You to Become a Teacher?"

A Desire to Make a Difference

Award recipients shared stories and passions, describing the inspirations that set them on their professional paths to the classroom. The most frequently cited reason for teaching in a community college was the quintessential human response: the desire to make a difference. We begin with one observation embraced and expressed the collective thoughts:

I'm an addicted "door opener." So many students can only see the walls; others find the door but are afraid to knock or even touch the knob. I know I can oil the locks and coach students to open the doors. Not all will walk through, but the joy of following students as they launch themselves into new worlds is addictive, indeed.
—Barbara Clinton, Highline Community College (WA)

I just hope that I can make a difference in someone's life.

I feel "called"—it was a process that circumstances proved was the right choice.

When I discovered that I couldn't save the world by practicing law, I thought I could at least make a contribution to the world by teaching.

A community college education is life-changing—what better place to make a difference with my one and only life?

I have had a very successful career in industry. I feel it is now time to "give back" to the next generation. This is my opportunity.

I have an abiding interest in "making a difference" in people's lives—helping students go from living in a car with their kids to a valued career with self-esteem and independence.

I was a 60s activist who decided to go to the classroom in the 80s. I can still be an activist!

Education was a way for me to find a better life. I want to help others do the same.

I've always wanted to be a teacher because I want to give back to society what my teachers gave me.

As one from a poor family and ethnic group, I wanted to help others break out of the poverty/welfare lifestyle/rut.

I want to champion those whose talents might be less obvious or somehow under-appreciated.

I'm busy changing the world one person at a time.

I am in the unique position of molding the leaders of tomorrow because they are in my classroom today.

I have always wanted to serve in one way or another. Teaching is a great challenge; I plan on retiring the year I finally do it all "right."

I wanted to learn more and to change my world for the better by helping others to do the same.

The Loves of Our Lives

Barbara Clinton's remark is a compelling, appropriate launching pad from which to explore several other inspirations that the study participants described in four different response categories, all ranking in the top 6. And, if considered as a collection of "loves of our lives," it overwhelms—actually, embraces—the notion of making a difference.

> *When we truly care for ourselves, it becomes possible to care far more profoundly*
> *about other people. The more alert and sensitive we are to our own needs, the more loving*
> *and generous we can be toward others.*
> —Eda LeShan

Love of the Subject

I taught for a few years, then I felt that I needed real-world experiences. I worked in business for 15 years, then returned to teaching with examples and stories galore.

I love math and want others to love it.

Literature gives us context and breadth.

Love of Learning

Students are fun. There is the joy of learning and the sharing of curiosity.

Learning is realizing the opportunity to be always changing.

I enjoy being a student myself.

I remember the excitement and joy in the undergraduate courses I took—where we country, small-town people were shown the world of Chaucer, Shakespeare, and Hawthorne.

I love learning and love taking classes; I get bored with the repetition of a job, doing the same task over and over. In teaching, this is an asset.

I spent many hours playing "school" as a child.

Love of People

I like interaction with people.

I enjoy the excitement of meeting new students.

What inspires me to continue being a teacher, with the imprecision of it all—I love it! It is wonderfully messy and human. I think I need this heightened contact in my life—a certain equation of hot-house feeling, connecting, and growing.

I like the human interaction. I teach in an area (art) where only humans can do the work and each one can do it differently. There are few chances to have that situation. Teaching and reinforcing the value of the humanities is one such chance.

I wasn't inspired in the beginning. I was inspired by students once I got there.

I want to help individual students become better human beings, sensitive to other humans' needs; to grow as people, to be productive members of society; to respect other individuals and accept them the way they are. I want them to learn to function in a pluralistic, multicultural society.

Love of Teaching

I was born with chalk dust in my blood!

I remember my excitement at getting my first library card and discovering that I could learn anything I wanted to from books.

Where else can you inform, entertain, direct, guide, counsel, learn from—all simultaneously!

The thrill of seeing the eyes light up, reflect; the student learning something new; none of that has diminished from the first time I saw it in my young brothers and sisters.

I enjoy the excitement of the new beginning of each new semester.

I was born to teach!

I guess it's just in me—I'm a stage director. In Greek, the word for director is "didaskalos"; it really means teacher.

I became a teacher almost by assumption (in my field) or by accident. I stayed a teacher because it's an honorable and rewarding way to spend one's work life—sound hokey? It's me!

I tried it and fell in love! There is no better place for constant job satisfaction.

It's so damned much fun!

I wasn't inspired; I evolved! It became something I am good at doing.

I've always had a desire to teach; when we played "school," I was always the teacher.

I knew I was good at school; I figured I could be a good teacher.

I just loved to watch people "get it."

Personal Benefits

There are so many intrinsic and extrinsic rewards.

I enjoy having control of my life.

The autonomy I have with this job makes it special.

The schedule is terrific—especially for a "mom."

Teaching gives me a place where I can be in charge—and responsible.

I'm a natural show-off!

I enjoyed being the star of the show—I have a captive audience for my jokes.

I am delighted to have had a mid-life career crisis as an industrial manager; otherwise, I would not have found this one.

I am glad to have discovered a safe place where I had to work to lose respect rather than work to gain it!

I am a frustrated comedian—I like being "on stage."

I became a college teacher because I had my own young children and needed my world to be more than two feet tall!

I enjoy having summers off—a chance to spend most of the year helping others although having some time for me to continue learning and growing.

I like the variety of experiences every day.

Serendipity

Respondents talked about the various pleasures associated with anticipating and embracing the serendipity in life, and many observed that serendipity was responsible for their being in the classroom.

The soul should always stand ajar, ready to welcome the ecstatic experience.
—Emily Dickinson

I was forced into the classroom as a teaching assistant.

It was by accident. We needed a sociology teacher to fill an adjunct class; I taught it. I never wanted to go back to administration. That was more than 30 years ago.

I believe in the magical, mystical theory of "vocational choice." I "fell" into it!

I became a teacher by accident. I was an Architectural Engineering student and began teaching to help pay my tuition. I changed my major to pure mathematics and remained in teaching.

An unplanned opportunity. I still bless the woman who quit without notice. Her leaving the classroom gave me an opportunity to teach for a year. I'd never thought I wanted to teach, but I discovered that I LOVED it!

I was "downsized" in banking (something I did well but didn't love) and looked for something I could love and "make a difference."

I became a teacher by default; it was an available job when I moved back to my home-town; but I remained a teacher because I love to see the "lights go on" in students.

My department chair asked me to teach after graduation. He had more vision than I did at the time—I tried it! I liked it!! I live it!!! I love it!!!!

I never wanted to be a teacher but made it my back-up plan. When the back-up plan became necessary, I found that teaching was my real love!

In junior high school, the principal asked me to tutor a 4th grader, whose mother had called the school and made a request for tutoring. I enjoyed that experience so much, that I thought I'd like to do it "forever."

Somebody needed a teacher fast—and then I found my soul!

Positive Role Models, Family, Friends, and Significant Others

Although the following responses are taken from two different categories of responses, we group them together because they represent the same concept: attending to the advice and passion of others.

A great teacher made me want to be one!

A wonder woman professor, when I returned at 32—I had never thought of a woman as a professor!

My fifth-grade teacher!

A fifth-grade teacher believed in me and built up my self-esteem—even though her teaching methods were very traditional.

Flattery and persuasion—one counselor and two faculty were urging me to become a teacher.

The professor I worked for as an (old) TA so loved his students.

I was lured into teaching by a mentor who saw what I did not yet see.

A high school teacher seemed "inspired" about life and learning. She had such a profound effect on me as a human being to "care" about others. Wanted to be that kind of inspiration to others.

Positive relationships with caring teachers in grammar and high school.

Some of the most memorable teachers I had as role models from kindergarten through the university. (I can even tell you all of their names!)

As a sophomore in high school, I was inspired by my English teacher; he taught both content and life, and he displayed a wonderful, sincere concern for each student as an individual. I am now an English instructor!

I was fortunate to have a series of good teachers who inspired (meaning: "kicked my ass" into developing what ability I had) me to be successful.

Excellence-dedicated humanists who were my teachers on all levels and who inspired me to continue their work.

The history teacher in my first year of college was great. You know what? He was a lecturer!!!

Teachers were my role models as I was growing up. They loved me, encouraged me, scolded me, and guided me.

A person that I respected told me that I would be good at it! So I changed careers, and LIFE IS GOOD!!!

Throughout my life, people kept telling me that I'd make a good teacher! Finally, I tried it—at age 43!

My father's dream for me was to get married and be a housewife. However, in case it should ever be necessary that I work, he encouraged me to teach. How times have changed!

I came from a family of teachers/learners: grandmother, mother, and aunt.
My father inspired me to become a teacher. Since I was a child, he always told me that it was the most rewarding career of all!

I'm the child of immigrant families. I knew my parents' stories. I feel familiar with and also always amazed by my students' stories and never somehow made hopeless by them. Who am I in this? I feel in an historical line with those who taught the outsiders a longing to learn.

Other people did. My mother said of me (what her mother said of her): "You could teach a bear to dance." I received definitions of and affirmations of my teaching abilities from the time I was a girl.

My mother asked me whether I wanted to be a teacher or a nurse. I didn't like blood, so I selected teaching…I found I loved it.

I had a great aunt who was one of the first female superintendents in the state of Ohio. Her love and patience with others were tremendous inspirations.

Someone at some point told me I was good at my job (secretary) and should teach/tell others how to do it more effectively.

Negative Role Models

There were a number of respondents who talked openly about the power of negative role models on their decisions to teach and how they especially influenced them to aim for being the best teachers they could be.

A staff person in high school told me that I would never go beyond high school.

My own lousy teachers.

When I started teaching, I promised myself that I would never treat students as I had been treated!

I have a desire to give to others that which I had never received from my teachers.

In law school, I had a very bad instructor. I vowed that if I ever taught, I would be completely unlike him.

I hated school! I wanted to make it better for others.

Conclusion

We close this chapter with another compelling, true story. In May 1992, during the Excellence Awards celebration at the close of NISOD's annual conference, two award recipients recognized each other across a crowded section of honorees, their friends and colleagues. The two signaled that they should meet outside the auditorium at the close of the session. Who were they? They were each award recipients at their respective colleges, and they had not seen the other in more than 25 years—one had taught the other! The former student, now a teacher, stopped by after their meeting to tell us about the serendipity of that event, the emotional reunion, and the pride they shared in their work of making a difference in the lives of their students. They observed that their journey had come full circle on that special day.

It is good to have an end to journey toward; but it is the journey that matters in the end.
—Ursula K. LeGuin

What we learned from award recipients who spoke passionately about their journeys toward teaching is that no matter where their paths to teaching may have begun, or what routes they took, it was the process of making their way to the classroom that they valued. Our only regret is that we did not ask them directly why they stay. Perhaps their answers are better woven throughout the remaining chapters of this book. But in their discussions at this juncture, they underscored the human dimension of this enterprise and applauded Terry O'Banion's notion that a shared journey is the best journey of all.

Chapter Four

Historical Overview of Teaching Excellence

Community college faculty will always have to deal with new kinds of students, reach beyond the teaching strategies they began with. This has been true for at least thirty years. It promises to be even truer in the coming years.

—Griffith and Connor (1994, p. 65)

Even with the explosion of information technology (IT) and education reform efforts, one can still compellingly argue that teachers remain linchpins in our educational system. They are often virtual flash points in students' lives. When the subject to be taught is intriguing and enormously interesting to the majority of students in a class, then teachers' personalities and behaviors may not be so obvious—unless, of course, they are able to kill the subject, along with the spirits of the students! However, when the material is less attractive and not so engaging early on, then teachers' abilities to engage students can literally carry the day and determine how well students embrace the subject and how excited they become about their own learning. Good teachers mold and shape students' attitudes about what they can be and do. Good teachers affect and effect learning at every level.

This is all good to say, but what we know about what teachers report and what they actually *do*—especially excellent teachers—drives what we look for, what we ask about, and what we describe when we investigate excellent teaching practices and models. We offer this historical preface to and a context for chapter 5, in which we report on what excellent teachers say about what they believe constitutes successful teaching and how they do it to effect learning as they teach content. This overview also revisits familiar educational landmarks that—whether studied as methods or theories, or abided by philosophically or for practicality—mark the various pathways that have been created by continuing interests in and with the intentions of improving teaching and learning.

Historical Landmarks and Hallmarks

The walls of teacher education classrooms have at one time or another been decorated with posters depicting various teaching situations, many carrying dire warnings—arguably, the most memorable: "We never said teaching would be *easy!*" This pronouncement is emphasized further by graphic pictures of exhausted teachers, frustrated or out-of-control students, or disorganized stacks of papers on the teacher's desk caught in mid-air on their slide to top off the piles of papers already on the floor. And, many teachers, once employed and in the classroom, observed that this warning was understated!

Yet, a well-documented body of literature pronounces and confirms numerous reports, observations, and other related data that good teaching survives even the most enormous and horrendous challenges, that good teaching is alive and well at all levels of education. It continues that good teaching is supported, primarily, by the behaviors of teaching professionals who care enough to ignore the warnings of "tough job" and respond with abandon to the serious challenges that are part and parcel of teaching at any level.

The researchers and educators who wrote *A Nation at Risk* listed a number of tools that were available to assist in the education reform that they proposed, among them "the dedication, against all odds, that keeps teachers serving in schools and colleges, even as the rewards diminish" (National Commission on Excellence in Education, 1983, p. 15). This report documented that teachers have not given up and that they will not do so any time soon. Evidence abounds that good teaching is neither dead nor dying in public schools, colleges, and universities (Roueche & Baker, 1986, 1987). And, as the stakes in student success climb higher, we are more compelled than ever to expect, support, and encourage teaching performance that goes far beyond good—that aims for and achieves excellence.

From our seats as former students, researchers, and "naïve observers" (Cross, 1994, p. 684) of classroom practices, the majority of current educators can readily identify characteristics of teaching excellence. We instinctively distinguish the mediocre professor from the master and the lifeless, perfunctory class from the animated and inspired. We can easily spot the professor who has real "fire in her belly" for her subject and the professor who opens our textbooks along with our hearts. Nevertheless, what it means to be an exemplary college teacher is a difficult concept to capture in research terms and one that has been long and often hotly debated by scholars as well as practitioners.

Some argue that good teachers—or rather, as better fits this discussion, excellent teachers—are born, not made (Kelley & Wilbur, 1970). Some place the essence of teaching excellence in the personality of the person (Pullias, 1963). Others characterize exemplary teachers as artists, marked by distinctive natural styles, each having his or her own excellence that fits particular definitions of relevance (Axelrod, 1970). Some describe the science underlying the art of teaching and characterize teaching exemplars as good scientists (Gage, 1978), or argue that teaching excellence is best achieved by developing one's craft—an honest, practiced, yet creative endeavor (Eble, 1976, 1983).

Still others take issue with the inquiry altogether and claim that "the question should not be 'What is the ideal college teacher?' but rather 'What is the ideal college teacher for different contexts (i.e., courses, students, and settings) and different goals, objectives or desired outcomes of instruction?'" (Abrami, 1985, p. 224). Such divergent perspectives about the focus and results of research on teaching effectiveness have enriched the literature and offered practitioners, in particular, a rich descriptive array of characteristics and practices of exemplary college teachers and contributed to a growing conceptual understanding of how these attributes and actions lead to improved teaching and more successful learning.

What We Have Learned About Effective Undergraduate Teaching

The question of what it means to be an effective college teacher has been the focus of study in this country for at least 70 years (Arreola, 1995; McKeachie, 1990). Over the last 15 years in particular, reviews of this literature on instruction in higher education report that studies vary widely and extensively in method, focus, and quality (see, e.g., Cole, 1982; Ellner & Barnes, 1983; McKeachie, 1990; Svinicki, Hagen, & Meyer, 1996). Most reviewers concur with Svinicki et al. (1996, p. 257) that this literature is "both vast and sparse: vast in that there are thousands of articles on ways to teach, and sparse because many of them contribute little in the way of reliable, generalizable information that has been empirically verified."

Nevertheless, McKeachie's 1990 historical survey of the experimental research on college teaching confirms that this body of research has developed sufficiently to meet the classic criteria (established by J. B. Conant in 1937) for a field of study to be considered scientific—accumulation of knowledge in the field and development of new conceptual scheme based on experiments and observations that, in turn, spawn further research in the field. McKeachie asserted that, despite the inherent challenge in studying such a complex and controversial endeavor as college teaching, this evolving body of research has made meaningful contributions to educational practice and will continue to do so:

We now know learning skills and strategies that generally help students to learn more effectively…We now know that intrinsic motivation and a sense of self-efficacy have much to do with learning strategies.…We now know more about the processes leading toward educational outcomes.…We now know that students can evaluate teaching effectiveness.…We now know that educational research can be of practical help to faculty members and institutions; in the next decade we will better understand how to avoid the misuse of research and how to get more effective links to practice. (McKeachie, 1990, p. 197)

The extensive literature derived from research on college teaching effectiveness provides an array of perspectives regarding what constitutes good undergraduate teaching. There are literally thousands of studies and reports that approach effectiveness from every angle imaginable. We touch on only a fraction of them here as we observe that comparative reviews of hundreds of these studies find considerable agreement among students, colleagues, administrators, alumni, and external researchers regarding what constitutes effective teaching (Centra, 1996; Lowman, 1996; Seldin, 1988). This collection of research findings confirms Eble's (1972, p. 29) assertion, made more than 25 years ago, that "what makes an effective or ineffective teacher can be identified, profitably discussed, and fairly evaluated." Here we will provide a brief examination of findings from two categories of this body of research: successful college teaching methods and typologies of best practices in undergraduate education.

I am a pluralist. I cannot conceive of any one way of teaching that will excel all others.
—Eble (1976, p. 4)

Successful College Teaching Methods

The literature on successful teaching methods for undergraduate education runs the gamut from scholarly discussions based on well-documented experience (e.g., Eble, 1976, on teaching as craft) to rigorous empirical analyses of effective teaching strategies (e.g., McKeachie, 1990, 1994). A number of reviewers have examined and scrutinized this literature, principally for purposes of improving college teaching effectiveness. Eble (1976) reviewed findings on traditional techniques such as lecture as discourse, discussion, seminars, tutorials, and advising. Svinicki et al. (1996) summarized findings on six higher education instructional methods—lecture, discussion, cooperative learning, problem-based methods, mastery methods, and computer-based methods. McKeachie's (1994) classic, *Teaching Tips: Strategies, Research, and Theory for College and University Teachers,* has guided faculty and teaching assistants since 1951 on a wide spectrum of college teaching strategies spanning lecture, discussion, writing, laboratory teaching, fieldwork, peer learning, project methods, case method, independent study, instructional games, role playing, and electronic learning tools. We will limit our discussion here to a small collection of research findings related to five of the most common instructional methods used effectively in undergraduate teaching: *lecture, discussion, collaborative learning,* and *computer-enabled learning.*

Lecture is an unnatural act, an act for which providence did not design humans. It is perfectly all right, now and then, for a human to be possessed by the urge to speak, and to speak although others remain silent. But to do this regularly, one hour and 15 minutes at a time…for one person to drone on although others sit in silence?…I do not believe that this is what the Creator…designed humans to do.
—Patricia Limerick (cited in Smith, 1990, p. 210)

Lecture

Even with the range of emotions associated with lecture as a teaching strategy, it has been the coin of the realm of teaching for centuries. Despite the advent of the printed word in the Western world, television and videos in recent memory, and the World Wide Web in the last decade, the lecture remains the staple of undergraduate teaching (McKeachie, 1994). Notwithstanding its pedagogical stronghold, consistent empirical evidence underscores the lecture's shortcomings for providing long-term or high-level learning. Our growing understanding of cognitive learning processes provides insights into what happens to learners in lecture situations. Peter Senge, director of the Center for Organizational Learning at Massachusetts Institute of Technology, explained it this way:

> Really deep learning is a process that inevitably is driven by the learner, not by someone else. And it always involves moving back and forth between a domain of thinking and a domain of action. So having a student sit passively taking in information is hardly a very good model for learning; it's just what we're used to. (cited in O'Neil, 1995, p. 20)

Repeated studies demonstrate that lecture is a relatively effective method of instruction for immediate recall of factual information, but less effective than discussion, peer learning, or self-paced learning methods for long-term retention or higher-order learning, such as comprehension or application (McKeachie, 1990). However, it is important that before decrying the use of lecture, one should at least "recognize [its] basic attractiveness" (Eble, 1976, p. 43). "For the most part, teachers…enter into lecturing too lightly, pay too little attention to what good lectures might accomplish" (p. 44). No instructional system yet contrived offers the same combination of expedient and inexpensive delivery of information with personal involvement on the part of teacher and student. Lectures are useful for summarizing material from a variety of sources, conveying current information and research that may not be available in other media, providing structure for student learning, stimulating student interest and motivation, and instructor modeling of problem solving, critical thinking, and scholarship (McKeachie, 1994). Based on decades of research and personal observation of hundreds of college classrooms, Eble (1976) not only defended the lecture but also offered advice on its efficacious use:

> Delivered by a professor with a high degree of competence, classroom lectures may well achieve the objectives peculiar to their substance and impact: conveying information to a large audience with some expectation that this information is being received, and stimulating students to pursue specific or related learning on their own. (p. 43)

Exemplary college faculty members use a variety of techniques to enhance the effectiveness of their lectures (Davis, 1976; Eble, 1976; Feldman, 1988; McKeachie, 1994; Pascarella & Terenzini, 1991; Roueche et al., 1997; Svinicki et al., 1996). They carefully organize the course material and make learning objectives clear. They maximize student interest and attention by using enthusiasm, humor, movement, audio-visual aids, and by varying the pitch, intensity, and pace of the lecture. They increase clarity and understanding by using illustrations and examples, signaling key points and topic shifts, asking questions to check for comprehension, and periodically summarizing information. They engage students in active writing, thinking, or discussion activities during the lecture. They are alert to students through verbal and nonverbal cues and adjust their presentation in reference to such student feedback. In sum, effective college teachers recognize the strengths and weaknesses of the lecture method and use it strategically as only one of many tools in their teaching repertoire.

Discussion

Researchers comparing lecture with discussion have demonstrated little difference between these teaching strategies in terms of immediate recall, but have found discussion methods superior in terms of long-term retention, problem solving, critical thinking outcomes, and positive affect toward the subject *if done well* (Eble, 1976; McKeachie, 1990; Svinicki et al., 1996). Discussion methods are consistent with what cognitive learning researchers identify as *deep processing*—learning aimed at constructing meaning by relating new information to prior knowledge or organizing content into structures—in contrast to *surface processing*—simply reproducing or memorizing new information (Jackson, 1995; McKeachie, 1990). Discussion methods are less effective than lectures for presenting new information but are more effective for clarifying information, raising the level of student involvement in the classroom, providing feedback about student progress and attitudes, and developing individual skills of formulating and expressing ideas and opinions (Eble, 1976). Successful use of discussion in undergraduate classrooms calls for significant skills in effective group facilitation to overcome the common challenges of nonparticipation, discussion monopolizers, student perceptions of non-progress in learning, and emotional reactions to conflicts that arise during discussions (McKeachie, 1994).

Exemplary college faculty integrate discussion methods in a variety of small- and large-group settings to engage students in interacting with concepts or skills being presented. They recognize that having students actively participate in the learning process deepens students' understanding, so they step out of the limelight and encourage students to think about and share their ideas about course topics. At the same time, they recognize challenges associated with student discussions and work to facilitate democratic participation, relevant dialogue, good listening skills, and achievement of learning goals within the sometimes chaotic environment that lively discussion creates. Cross (2002) further clarified these admonitions, noting the importance of and outlining strategies for using "learning-centered" classroom discussions. She argued that discussions should not only meet participatory and democratic ideals, but first and foremost lead toward deeper learning. Moreover, faculty members should assess the outcomes of discussion to see if they are leading toward greater understanding. Given the variety of discussion formats and strategies available, being tough-mindedly learning-centered allows this teaching technique to be thoughtfully and effectively utilized.

Collaborative Learning

Increasingly, effective college faculty are turning to collaborative learning methods to facilitate a shift to learner-centered instruction. Peer learning, cooperative learning, and collaborative learning are discussed in the literature as variations of students learning together in small groups. Although collaborative learning approaches have received significant attention in recent years (Cross, 2000; Cross & Angelo, 1988; O'Banion, 1998; Sticht & McDonald, 1989; Svinicki et al., 1996), these learning models were first popularized in the 1970s; and significant research has been conducted on a wide range of these models. McKeachie (1994), who has researched teaching effectiveness for more than 40 years, concluded that collaborative learning is more effective than many other forms of learning:

> The best answer to the question, "What is the most effective method of teaching?" is that it depends on the goal, the student, the content, and the teacher, but the next best answer is, "Students teaching other students." There is a wealth of evidence that peer learning and teaching is extremely effective for a wide range of goals, content, and students of different levels and personalities. (p. 144)

Socially organized, task-oriented activities—occurring in and out of class—in which students can talk about what they have learned are critical to improved skill development and application (Sticht & McDonald, 1989). Examples of such activities reflect the power of students working in pairs and in larger groups—they improve long- and short-term memories, increase students' interests in continuing other work in similar content areas (Light, 1990; Ullom, 1989), and improve language development (particularly in the case of native and foreign-born students working together on language acquisition and improvement) (Friedlander & MacDougall, 1992).

One unique model, a curricular structure referred to as learning communities, benefits teachers and students through collaborative learning activities and team teaching (Cross, 1999; Gabelnick, MacGregor, Matthews, & Smith, 1990—for an especially useful summary of the five major models; O'Banion, 1997; Pascarella & Terenzini, 1991). There are different models currently being implemented; however, in linking courses and cohorts of students, colleges engage and keep students involved with the institution, teachers, and other students. Research tells us that engagement is the key to student retention (Cross, 1998; O'Banion, 1997; Tinto, 1987). Using the curriculum to design and support social engagement activities is a critical, proven-to-be-successful teaching and retention strategy; and it may well be the best strategy for helping students fold significant social engagement with the academic community into their busy lives with limited space and time for extracurricular pursuits.

The gee-whiz futurists are always wrong because they believe technological innovation travels in a straight line. It doesn't. It weaves and bobs and lurches and sputters.
—Naisbitt (1982, p. 41)

Computer-Enabled Learning

This picture repeats itself in some of the most visible changes in instruction—that of computer applications to improving teaching and learning (Bell, 1991; O'Banion, 1989). Early on, the application of computers to instruction was "merely *independent* study of the same …dominated by the behaviorists' model of reinforcement and repetition (Anandam, 1989, p. 109), or computer-assisted instruction that was more "responding" then "using" them (Shaw, 1989), or "to use technology for *individualizing* the learning environment" (Anandam, 1989, p. 109). Today, there is ample evidence that we have achieved an application level with technology on which "what a student learns is no longer separate from how he or she learns.…[t]echnology now demands integration of method and content" (Shaw, 1989, p. 33). Today's students not only learn new content—that can help blur the usually sharp and distinct lines between disciplines—through technology, but they "learn the technology" (Roueche & Roueche, 1993, p. 178).

As the technology becomes more sophisticated, so do the opportunities it offers to improve student learning. Svinicki et al. (1996) predicted, however, that "this instructional tool will continue to outpace our ability to design uses for it and conduct research to test its effectiveness" (p. 271). Research inquiries are beginning to lay some useful foundations for further studies about the future of this learning tool, and they indicate that expanding capabilities will encourage and support greater creativity in instructional design. For example, communication between instructors and students and among students is improved and expanded with bulletin boards, chat rooms, networking activities, and the like.

Moreover, the nature of computer-enabled instruction lends itself to studies of the learning process itself—that is, we can begin to develop some probing questions, such as the following: What is the appropriate sequencing of materials? Should students' abilities, prior performance, experiences, and the like determine how much control they have over the pace and level of difficulty? Can studies of computer-enabled instruction help us design better strategies for responding to the barriers to learning that students bring to a subject or course? For example, students forced to delay their responses to a computer-generated question by at least 30 seconds formulated better answers than students who were allowed to respond at any time (Stokes, Halcomb, & Slovacek, 1988); students required to create and type in their own answers performed better than students who merely read the material and responded to the test question (Tudor & Bostow, 1991).

Since these early studies, more current applications of information technology indicate that cooperative learning activities via intranets and the Internet can direct and monitor the activities and progress of multiple students in collaborative learning groups. Of course, discussions about computer-enabled instruction must be tempered and extended by current dialogues about the infusion of a wide variety of new and emerging technologies in education—particularly in community colleges (Milliron & Miles, 2000). We will delve into these complex issues in much greater depth in chapter 8, where we explore the use of technology by teaching excellence award recipients.

Typologies of Best Practices in Undergraduate Education

> Teaching and learning are such complex processes, and teachers and learners are such complex beings, that no model of practice or pedagogical approach will apply in all settings. A lot of fruitless time and energy can be spent trying to find the holy grail of pedagogy, the one way to instructional enlightenment. No philosophy, theory, or theorist can possibly capture the idiosyncratic reality of your own experience as a teacher. Don't think that Freire, Dewey, Tyler, Rogers, or anyone else possesses the truth that fits your situation exactly. (Brookfield, 1990, p. 197)

In an extensive meta-analysis of student ratings of teaching, Feldman (1976) found nine characteristics that were related to high faculty ratings in almost all studies of teaching effectiveness: knowledge of subject, course preparation and organization, clarity and understandability, enthusiasm for subject/teaching, concern for students, availability and helpfulness, quality of examinations, impartiality in evaluating students, and overall fairness to students. The focus of research on college teaching has shifted significantly over the years from early studies of the impact of class size, the accuracy of student ratings of instruction, and the relative effectiveness of lecture versus discussion, to more recent investigations into interactions between teacher and student learning styles, and the effects of computer-based or cooperative learning strategies. Our most recent review of research on college teaching effectiveness confirms McKeachie's assessment of progress in the field. We found three major areas of development in research on college teaching: *conceptual progress* related to evolving models of learning and teaching, *methodological progress* through advances in psychometric principles and research design, and *progress in application to practice,* largely associated with new definitions of scholarship and accountability in higher education.

Conceptual Progress

Concepts of what constitutes effective college teaching are derived largely from theories of learning. No simple definition or unifying theory of learning exists, in part because of differing assumptions or perspectives within the field of learning. Learning has been variously viewed as training of the mind, gathering of knowledge, a process of individual development, a mechanistic change in behavior, and the development of insights resulting from interactions with one's environment (Cole, 1982). In the last half century, learning theory has changed significantly, and several major developments in conceptions of learning have directly influenced college teaching research: cognitive learning theory, adult learning theory, student-centered learning theory, and learning-centered theory.

Cognitive learning theory. Early research on college teaching is rooted in the pioneering work of Skinner on behaviorism (1938, 1953, 1968), in which learning is conceived as changes in behavior in response to external stimuli. During the 1930s and 1940s, behaviorists sought to establish general theories of behavior based on learning, such as Clark Hull's hypothetico-deductive system and E. L. Thorndike's trial-and-error learning models, which although unsuccessful, stimulated much inquiry into problems and issues of learning in higher education (Fincher, 1994). College teaching research in this period focused on analyzing behavioral responses (typically student test performance) to varying stimuli (e.g., teaching methods, differences in class sizes).

Beginning in the 1950s, research on learning began to shift toward a more cognitive focus on knowledge and how it is acquired and used. Researchers began looking at the learning process itself and identifying not only different stages of learning, but also different types of learning. The most widely accepted classification of learning proposed during this period was the hierarchical categorization of educational objectives in the cognitive domain offered by Bloom (1956)—knowledge, comprehension, application, analysis, synthesis, and evaluation—followed by a comparable taxonomy for the affective domain (Krathwohl, Bloom, & Masia, 1964). Although these taxonomies were developed by a committee of college and university examiners to assist faculty members in assessing course objectives (McKeachie, 1994) and were widely discussed among college faculty (Fincher, 1994), most studies of cognitive levels used in classrooms have been conducted at the pre-college level.

As cognitive learning theories gained widespread acceptance during the 1960s and 1970s, more researchers shifted their focus from the teacher to the learner, and new research began documenting how learners are active participants in constructing their own understanding and learning. Research applying cognitive theories to learning in college has taken a variety of paths, including investigations of effects of personality and motivation on learning, and studies on individual skills, strategies, and styles of learning (Brown & Atkins, 1988). In addition to generating new research paths, cognitive learning theories have provided a conceptual base for understanding results of earlier studies. For example, cognitive research explains that smaller classes and discussion methods tend to be effective because students are actively processing information rather than passively listening. McKeachie (1990) summarized the effects of cognitive theories on college teaching research: "We now realize that the variables influencing learning are almost numberless....The frontier of knowledge about college teaching thus becomes even more challenging" (p.197).

Adult learning theory. One outgrowth of cognitive learning theory with particular salience to college teaching research has been the development of specific theories of adult learning. One of the first researchers to recognize that adults represent a unique group of learners was Malcolm Knowles (1973), who argued for a more relevant and self-directed model of teaching for adults, which he termed "andragogy." Andragogy is based on four assumptions regarding adult learners: (1) as people mature, they become increasingly self-directed; (2) adults have an experience base that facilitates new learning; (3) the readiness of an adult student to learn relates more to preparation for social tasks than to biological development; and (4) adults tend to have a problem-centered orientation to learning.

Brookfield (1994) found the research related to adult learning to be extensive: "Judging by the number of journal articles, dissertations, and studies devoted to it, the topic of participation in adult learning is probably the most enduring research concern since investigations of this field began" (p. 138). Although adult learning theory has been criticized by researchers, primarily for problems with application (Cranton, 1994), a significant body of this research suggests that adults seem to learn most effectively when they actively participate in the educational experience, set their own learning pace, and perceive the learning topic to be immediately relevant to their lives (Brookfield, 1986, 1994; Cole, 1982; Cross, 1981; Knowles, 1973; Knox, 1977). This body of research has substantially influenced discussions around moving away from teacher-centered to student-centered or self-directed learning in college classrooms.

Student-centered learning theory. Both cognitive learning theory and adult learning theory have influenced significant discussions regarding learning activities, variously referred to as student-centered, learner-centered, and self-directed learning perspectives. Early cognitive theorists, such as Jerome Bruner who in 1966 attributed high degrees of autonomy and initiative to individual learners, laid the groundwork for placing learners at center stage in college teaching: "Learners are not simply passive recipients of information; they actively construct their own understanding" (cited in Svinicki, 1991, p. 27).

McKeachie (1990) cited the effects on research of student-centered college teaching methods of the convergence of two independent movements in psychology—Carl Rogers's nondirective approach to counseling and Kurt Lewin's group dynamics movement. These perspectives "emphasized movement away from the teacher's role as expert and authority to a role of facilitating student responsibility for learning" (McKeachie, 1990, p. 191). Early research on student-centered approaches in the 1940s and 1950s found student-centered discussion methods equal to lecture methods in measures of student performance on course final examinations but generally assessed student-centered methods superior in other outcome measures, such as student motivation, attitude, or deeper understanding. More recent college teaching research has focused on independent study methods, active learning strategies, collaborative learning approaches, and computer-based instruction as applications of student-centered learning theory.

Learning-centered theory. This emerging body of literature (Barr & Tagg, 1995; Boggs, 1993; Cross, 2002; Milliron & Miles, 2000; O'Banion, 1997; O'Banion & Milliron, 2001) extends student-centered learning theory to the extent that it argues for the tough-minded analysis of all elements of the teaching and learning process to ask two key questions: (1) Do the policies, practices, procedures, and people in place improve and expand learning? and (2) How do you know? The essence of this perspective is that all too often teaching and learning practice is defined by history or convenience, not on whether or not the activities can track to improve learning. It can be argued that in many ways this is a meta-theory of learning, embracing many prior conceptual frameworks, but demanding results.

An unfortunate turn in learning-centered education emerged in the mid-1990s, with the publication of Barr and Tagg's article, "From Teaching to Learning: A New Paradigm for Undergraduate Education" (1995). Although they did a noteworthy job of outlining the challenges in the modern educational system, the core conceptual argument Barr and Tagg advanced was that the key challenge was a focus on teaching rather than on learning. The most violent rhetorical aspect of this debate was that often the word "teaching" became almost synonymous with "bad teaching." Whenever staff development professionals spoke of teaching, they evoked images of the worst of the profession, rather than the best. In often-justified bouts of frustration, many faculty rejected learning-centered education as disrespectful of their often clearly "learning-centered" efforts—seeing it as yet another hyperbole-filled reform concept. They could rightfully argue that the best faculty had always been learning-centered and that many of the deficiencies outlined by the critics were due to administrative or policy frameworks that were well beyond their control (Gonick & Milliron, 2002). Even more challenging than the false dichotomy between teaching versus learning, versus the "irrational exuberance" of the late 1990s dotcom explosions that adopted learning-centered education, arguing that information technology would be the savior for education and the true enabler of learning-centered education (Milliron & Johnson, 2002).

Given the dialectic and clearly symbiotic relationship between teaching and learning, key advocates of learning-centered education quickly labeled the teaching- versus learning-centered education a red-herring argument and have more recently begun clearly articulating the role of "teaching in a learning college" (Cross, 2002; Gonick & Milliron, 2002; Milliron & Leach, 1997, Milliron & Miles, 2000, O'Banion, 1997, O'Banion & Milliron, 2001, Wilson, 2002). Moreover, as a more realistic and rational exuberance about technology sets in, more educational professionals realize that this powerful tool can help in fostering and documenting learning-centered education. However, it is the thoughtful application of technology by teachers, leaders, and students that will lead to learning-centered education (Gonick & Milliron, 2002; Milliron, 2001; O'Banion & Milliron, 2001).

Methodological Progress

In the last several decades, the literature on college teaching has reflected a gradual movement away from prescriptive essays to reports of rigorously designed research of teaching effectiveness. Ellner and Barnes's (1983) review of studies of college teaching found the bulk of college teaching literature to be books and articles offering "helpful day-to-day advice and inspiration…[that] do not pretend to be based on a body of scientific knowledge" (p. 13). More than a decade later, Svinicki et al. (1996) found that college teaching literature was still dominated by non–research-based descriptive accounts of personal experiences with various teaching strategies, but they reported helpful trends in the application of empirical methods to college instruction research. These researchers found a growing body of empirically based studies of college teaching, including comparative studies of instructional strategies, analytic studies investigating "why" and "how" certain factors influence success or failure of a given strategy, and "derivative studies" (p. 259) that are idiosyncratic to particular instructional methods, such as students' social and intellectual development in collaborative learning environments.

Advances in research design. In his review of empirical studies of college teaching since the 1920s, McKeachie (1990) reported numerous topics related to college teaching, ranging from impact of class size, lecture versus discussion methods, efficacy of independent study and peer learning techniques, evaluation of teaching, and the effects of technology on teaching and learning. Methodologically, these studies evolved from simple evaluations of teaching effectiveness based on test score achievement to comprehensive meta-analyses of diverse findings from multiple studies for the purpose of identifying patterns.

An early development in research design was the use of *attribute-treatment interactions* in studies during the 1950s, which began considering relationships between variable student or teacher traits and learning outcomes, rather than single trait relationships (McKeachie, 1990). The consideration of how students or teachers with varying attributes (such as gender, age, major, socioeconomic status, years of experience, learning styles) interact with certain teaching approaches (or with each other) has become an integral aspect of what is considered to be good research design. Before the 1950s, however, college teaching research often focused on overall achievement of classes of students in response to given teaching approaches.

In the 1960s, process-product research—also known as process-outcome studies (Ellner & Barnes, 1983)—advanced college teaching research by moving toward more detailed analyses of complex classroom processes and their relationships to student outcomes. Process-product studies, such as the landmark *The College Classroom* (Mann et al., 1970)—detailing changes in teacher roles, student behaviors, and interactions of four introductory psychology courses over a semester—began to provide the college teaching literature with more in-depth understanding of the complex links between teaching processes and learning outcomes. A more recent study, *Teaching Within the Rhythms of the Semester* (Duffy & Jones, 1995), integrated many of the findings from process–product studies with findings from research on learning and teaching effectiveness to provide a developmental guide to college teaching.

In the late 1970s, meta-analysis methods began being applied to college teaching research. Meta-analysis, a quantitative analysis process in which researchers apply multivariate techniques to the findings from a large body of individual studies, allows researchers to compare findings across studies and helps correct for limitations in individual studies (Cole, 1982). From his review of more than 300 books and articles on instruction in higher education, Cole (1982, pp. 44–45) concluded that the development of meta-analysis was "the most significant development in the methodology of educational research."

The power of meta-analysis research is exemplified in studies of the effects of instructional technology on college students. Individual studies demonstrated mixed results, but a meta-analysis of 59 individual studies of computer-based undergraduate instruction demonstrated that this method makes small but significant contributions to achievement, has positive effects on student attitudes, and accomplishes learning tasks in less time than that required by conventional teaching methods (Kulik, Kulik, & Cohen, 1980). Nevertheless, this analysis revealed that the greatest successes with computer-based instruction were achieved with knowledge-based drill and practice programs.

Qualitative analysis. When Ellner and Barnes (1983) reviewed the status of studies on college teaching in 1983, they found little use of qualitative research methods. They argued that greater use of this research approach would contribute to better understanding of college teaching:

> Qualitative studies are appropriate means for studying college instruction when researchers wish to understand and interpret the whole of a reality in addition to its component parts....Since much instruction is situation-bound, influenced by student and institutional context as well as by the professor's biography and training, qualitative studies are able to incorporate these elements into its focus. (pp. 37–38)

Increasingly, process–product and case studies have incorporated qualitative data into their research designs. In the last decade, qualitative methods and combined qualitative and quantitative research approaches have been used in numerous studies of college teaching, adding significant descriptive, process, and contextual understanding to this body of literature (e.g., Baker et al., 1990; Barsi, 1991; Boice, 1991; Griffith & Connor, 1994; Higgins, Hawthorne, Cape, & Bell, 1994; Roueche & Roueche, 1993; Roueche, Roueche, & Milliron, 1995).

Linking Learning Theories to Teaching Practices

We are all too familiar with the polarization between college research and teaching practice. Increasing controversy over the lack of scholarship in teaching has spawned interest in research on processes of instruction and translation of research into policy and practice. In the past 10 years, two important changes in the relationship between research on college teaching and teaching practice have been brought to the forefront of the dialogue on teaching in college: new definitions of professorial scholarship that incorporate teaching excellence, and the application of new knowledge about learning to enhance learning outcomes in the college classroom.

New Definitions of Scholarship

The concept of scholarship predicated on discipline and research has been the standard in higher education for nearly a century (Paulsen & Feldman, 1995). Over the last decade, national calls for increasing the quality of education at all levels and a spate of publications decrying the state of undergraduate education in this country (e.g., Bloom, 1987; D'Souza, 1991; Hirsch, 1987; Smith, 1990) have called this traditional definition of scholarship into question. Much attention has been paid to the imbalance between the recognition and rewards accorded to teaching and research in higher education. In *Teaching Undergraduates*, Kimball (1988) described the capricious selection process for and lack of respect associated with the annual process of bestowing university teaching awards on faculty. He related the advice on teaching given him, only half-jokingly, by one of his graduate professors: "If you're in consideration for a teaching award, then you're doing something wrong" (p. 13).

Boyer (1987, 1990), who perhaps best synthesized the inconsistencies in faculty reward priorities in higher education, issued the call for an expanded definition of scholarship:

> A wide gap now exists between the myth and the reality of academic life. Almost all colleges pay lip service to the trilogy of teaching, research, and service, but when it comes to making judgments about professional per- formance, the three rarely are assigned equal merit....The time has come to move beyond the tired old "teaching versus research" debate and give the familiar and honorable term "scholarship" a broader, more capacious meaning, one that brings legitimacy to the full scope of academic work. (1990, p. 15)

Despite the persistence of institutional reward structures that favor research over teaching (Gomez-Mejia & Balkin, 1992; Tang & Chamberlain, 1997), a number of institutions are responding to Boyer's call for new definitions of scholarship to include activities that contribute directly to the improvement of teaching (Daly, 1994; Paulsen & Feldman, 1995; Roueche, Ely, & Roueche, 2001).

Guidelines for institutionalizing these new definitions of scholarship are documented in *Teaching on Solid Ground* (Menges, Weimer, & Associates, 1996), a publication of the National Center on Postsecondary Teaching, Learning, and Assessment, which posits three key processes inherent in a scholarly approach to improving college teaching: (1) systematic, reflective practice; (2) active inquiry about teaching and learning; and (3) intrinsic motivation. *Systematic, reflective practice,* popularized by Schön (1987), exemplifies a scholarly orientation to teaching by encouraging faculty to become more "instructionally aware," first, and to analyze, evaluate, and modify their daily practices of instruction, second (Weimer, 1996, p. 8). *Active inquiry about teaching and learning* encourages faculty to develop a "scholarly intrigue" (Weimer, 1996, p. 9) about teaching and learning. Such scholarly curiosity is epitomized in the use of classroom assessment techniques, championed by Angelo and Cross (1993), through which faculty systematically monitor student learning in the classroom and modify their teaching based on ongoing feedback from students. In this fashion, faculty create scholarly cycles of instructional improvement and help students become more self-directed, self-regulated learners.

The third process whereby faculty incorporate scholarship in teaching is through the powerful stimulation of *intrinsic motivation,* derived from applying the first two instructional processes. The combination of faculty actively focusing on student learning, developing knowledge and skills for promoting student success, and receiving frequent feedback about their activities is a powerful formula for motivation and commitment. A longtime researcher of intrinsic motivation, Csikszentmihalyi (1997) has asserted that intrinsically motivated enjoyment, or "flow," in teaching (as in any activity) is enhanced when goals are clear, feedback is immediate, a creative tension exists between one's skills and the challenges of the task, distractions are avoided, and control is possible: "an effective professor is one who is intrinsically motivated to learn, because it is he or she who will have the best chance to educate others" (p. 72).

Whereas faculty at four-year colleges and universities may struggle to embrace teaching under the umbrella of new definitions of scholarship, community college faculty are better situated to integrate the two traditionally separate faculty roles.

> Leading the discussion of changing scholarship concepts should be community college faculty members. Since they have defined their roles as teachers and not researchers, they are uniquely positioned within the higher education community to discuss, define, and fulfill the role of teacher-scholar. (Vaughan, 1994, 162)

Applying Learning Theories

A number of researchers have examined the transfer of learning theory to teaching practice and have offered inventories of "learning principles" to guide teaching improvement (e.g., American Psychological Association [APA], 1997; Angelo, 1993; Duffy & Jones, 1995; Katz & Henry, 1988; Svinicki et al., 1996). Perhaps the most fundamental of these are the "Learner-Centered Psychological Principles"—14 principles distilled by the American Psychological Association (APA) from a century of research on teaching and learning, with the specific goal of guiding American educational reform. Eleven of the 14 principles fall into three categories: (1) cognitive and metacognitive factors, (2) motivational and affective factors, and (3) developmental and social factors; the other three principles are categorized under "individual differences."

In Table 1, we compare APA's learning principles, Angelo's (1993) principles for improving higher education, and the general principles for teaching derived from cognitive learning theory identified by Svinicki et al. (1996). This comparative typology of research-based learning principles distills the wisdom and research findings from the multiple perspectives of psychologists, educators, and researchers, and it provides a comprehensive framework for translating learning theory to college teaching practice.

The overwhelming message from these three frameworks for linking theory to practice in higher education is that we should understand the cognitive, motivational, and social factors that influence learning—the "how" and "why" of learning—before considering the "what" of teaching practice. Svinicki et al. (1996) described how viewing teaching through the lens of learning theory will change how faculty approach the task of teaching:

> Rather than asking, what is the best instructional method for this content? [faculty] will wonder, Given what I know about learning, what should be included in my instruction, regardless of the particular instructional method I am using? (p. 282)

Table 1. Comparative Typology of Learning Principles

APA's Learner-Centered Principles (1997)	Angelo's "Teacher's Dozen" (1993)	Svinicki et al.'s Learning Principles (1996)
Cognitive Factors		
Nature of the learning process. The learning of complex subject matter is most effective when it is an intentional process of constructing meaning from information and experience.	**Attention and awareness.** Learning requires focused attention and awareness of the importance of what is to be learned.	**Attention.** Attention must be focused on critical information if learning is to take place. Attention is enhanced by offering variety, novelty, and interest value, highlighting, time spent on a topic, and appropriate context.
	Personal organization. Information organized in personally meaningful ways is more likely to be retained, learned, and used.	**Encoding and organization.** New information must be processed, structured, and connected in such a way as to be accessible in the future; this process is known as encoding. Good teaching practice incorporates a structured format that facilitates recall.
	Active learning. Active learning is more effective than passive learning. **Feedback.** To learn well, learners need feedback on their learning, early and often; to become independent, they need to learn how to give themselves feedback.	**Active, mindful involvement with feedback.** Learning will not take place until the learner does something to process the new information. This repeated and purposeful encoding, retrieval, and feedback gradually refines the learner's grasp of the content.

Table 1. Comparative Typology of Learning Principles (Cont'd)

APA's Learner-Centered Principles (1997)	Angelo's "Teacher's Dozen" (1993)	Svinicki et al.'s Learning Principles (1996)
Cognitive Factors		
Goals of the learning process. The successful learner, over time and with support and instructional guidance, can create meaningful, coherent representations of knowledge.	**Goals.** Learning is more effective and efficient when learners have explicit, reasonable, positive goals and when their goals fit well with the teacher's goals.	
Construction of knowledge. The successful learner can link new information with existing knowledge in meaningful ways.	**Prior knowledge.** To be remembered, new information must be meaningfully connected to prior knowledge; it must first be remembered to be learned. **Unlearning.** Unlearning what is already known is often more difficult than learning new information. **Mastery.** Mastering a skill or body of knowledge takes great amounts of time and effort. **Practice.** Learning to transfer, to apply previous knowledge and skills to new contexts, requires a great deal of practice.	**Activating prior knowledge.** Learning is enhanced by connecting what is known to what is being learned. Students benefit by having sufficient background information to understand the context of the subject being taught.
Strategic thinking. The successful learner can create and use a repertoire of thinking and reasoning strategies to achieve complex learning goals. **Thinking about thinking.** Higher order strategies for selecting and monitoring mental operations facilitate creative and critical thinking. **Context of learning.** Learning is influenced by environmental factors, including culture, technology, and instructional practices.		**Meta-cognition and self-regulation of learning.** How students think about their cognitions (meta-cognition) helps them become aware of the learning strategies necessary in different contexts and teaches them when and how to use those strategies.

Table 1. Comparative Typology of Learning Principles (Cont'd)

APA's Learner-Centered Principles (1997)	Angelo's "Teacher's Dozen" (1993)	Svinicki et al.'s Learning Principles (1996)
Motivational Factors		
Motivational and emotional influences on learning. What and how much is learned is influenced by the learner's motivation. Motivation to learn, in turn, is influenced by the individual's emotional states, beliefs, interest and goals, and habits of thinking.	**High expectations.** High expectations encourage high achievement. **Assessment.** The ways in which learners are assessed and evaluated powerfully affect the ways they study and learn.	**Motivation.** Motivation is what-ever activates and sustains goal-directed behavior in the learner, including qualities of the task, goal congruency, and characteristics of the learner.
Intrinsic motivation to learn. The learner's creativity, higher order thinking, and natural curiosity all contribute to motivation to learn. Intrinsic motivation is stimulated by tasks of optimal novelty and difficulty, relevant to personal interests, and providing for personal choice and control.	**Motivation to learn.** Motivation to learn is alterable; it can be positively or negatively affected by the task, the environment, the teacher, and the learner.	
Effects of motivation on effort. Acquisition of complex knowledge and skills requires extended learner effort and guided practice. Without learners' motivation to learn, the willingness to exert this effort is unlikely without coercion.	**Balance.** To be most effective, teachers need to balance levels of intellectual challenge and instructional support.	
Social Factors		
Developmental influences on learning. As individuals develop, there are different opportunities and constraints for learning. Learning is most effective when differential development within and across physical, intellectual, emotional, and social domains is taken into account.		
Social influences on learning. Learning is influenced by social interactions, interpersonal relations, and communication with others.	**Interaction with others.** Interaction between teachers and learners is one of the most powerful factors in promoting learning; interaction among learners is another.	

Table 1. Comparative Typology of Learning Principles (Cont'd)

APA's Learner-Centered Principles (1997)	Angelo's "Teacher's Dozen" (1993)	Svinicki et al.'s Learning Principles (1996)
Individual Factors		
Individual differences in learning. Learners have different strategies, approaches, and capabilities for learning that are a function of prior experience and heredity.		
Learning and diversity. Learning is most effective when differences in learners' linguistic, cultural, and social backgrounds are taken into account.		
Standards and assessment. Setting appropriately high and challenging standards and assessing the learner as well as learning progress—including diagnostic, process, and outcome assessment—are integral parts of the learning process.		

What constitutes good teaching practice in undergraduate education has been the focus of study over the last half century, and reports describe teachers as artists, scientists, or craftsmen—specifically, as drill masters, content-centered, instructor-centered, intellect-centered, or person-centered (Axelrod, 1970); content-oriented, process-oriented, or motivation-oriented (Menges, 1991); and disseminator/transmitters, inducer/persuaders, dialogists, or facilitator/guides (Duffy & Jones, 1995). Nevertheless, repeated studies indicate that no one style or orientation to teaching is superior to any other. In addition, research shows that faculty traits, such as age, gender, academic rank, and race, have little to do with teaching effectiveness (Bloom, 1980; Feldman, 1996). Cross (1994) pointed out that it is characteristics of *teaching,* rather than of *teachers,* which are found to differentiate between effectual and ineffectual teaching, at least from student perspectives.

Repeated studies of student and faculty assessment of college faculty reveal that teaching characteristics most highly correlated with effectiveness fall into three categories: intellectual competencies, motivational attributes, and interpersonal skills. From his extensive review of factor analysis studies on college teaching, coupled with his own study of superlative faculty as identified by students, faculty, and administrators, Lowman (1984) concluded that exemplary college teachers were those who excelled in at least one of two basic dimensions of college teaching (and were at least moderately competent in both dimensions): (1) skill at creating *intellectual excitement* and (2) strength in establishing *interpersonal rapport* with students.

Subsequent research with his Two-Dimensional Model of Effective College Teaching with data from three years of faculty and student descriptions of nominees for teaching awards at the University of North Carolina, Chapel Hill, revealed that the dimension of interpersonal rapport encompassed two subsets of teaching characteristics: (2a) behaviors communicating *interpersonal concern,* and (2b) skills for *motivating student learning* (Lowman, 1996).

These three resulting dimensions of exemplary college teaching—*intellectual excitement, interpersonal rapport,* and *skills for motivating student learning*—equate with the three categories of competencies of exemplary performance identified by Klemp (1977) from his study of individuals across a spectrum of career fields: *cognitive skills, interpersonal skills,* and *motivational skills.* It is important to note that these competencies—precursors of effective performance, as Klemp defines them—also mirror three categories of learner-centered psychological principles consistent with more than a century of research on teaching and learning: *cognitive/metacognitive factors, affective/motivational factors, and social factors* (APA, 1997). These three themes repeatedly appear in the literature on teaching effectiveness and form a robust triad of factors by which to assess excellence in college teaching (Baker et al., 1990; Lowman, 1996; Roueche & Baker, 1987; Thomas & Ferguson, 1987; Wilson, Gaff, Dienst, Wood, & Bavry, 1975).

In reviewing the literature of teaching excellence for the past 40 years, we found a number of researchers who have catalogued and validated best college teaching practices. Chickering and Gamson (1987) distilled findings from decades of research on undergraduate experience into "Seven Principles for Good Practice in Undergraduate Education." Roueche and Baker (1987) surveyed exemplary faculty at Miami-Dade Community College (FL) and organized 13 themes demonstrating excellent teaching practices around three categories derived from Klemp (1977). Feldman studied the relationships between student ratings and teaching effectiveness for more than two decades; his extensive meta-analysis of student's descriptions of effective teaching pointed up nine characteristics apparently related to high faculty ratings in almost all of the studies (1976, 1988).

In Table 2 we offer a comparative typology of good practices in college teaching that distills major findings and provides useful checkpoints as we analyze our participants' responses to our research questions regarding core strategies for effective teaching of content and of students.

Table 2. Comparative Typologies of Good Practice

Roueche and Baker's Teaching for Success Model (1987)	Chickering and Gamson's Seven Principles of Good Practice (1987)	Feldman's Nine Exemplary Teaching Characteristics (1988)
Intellectual Skills		
Individualized Perception. Excellent teachers recognize individual learning styles, interests, and motivations of students and adjust their courses to meet individual needs.	**Good practice respects diverse talents and ways of learning.** People bring different talents and styles of learning to college.	

Table 2. Comparative Typologies of Good Practice (Cont'd)

Roueche and Baker's Teaching for Success Model (1987)	Chickering and Gamson's Seven Principles of Good Practice (1987)	Feldman's Nine Exemplary Teaching Characteristics (1988)
Intellectual Skills (cont'd)		
Teaching Strategies. Excellent teachers activate students to think, to learn, to apply, to evaluate, to synthesize, and to grow through six major strategies: well-organized courses, student involvement, higher-order thinking skills, relevancy of application, use of monitoring and evaluation, and flexibility and variety in delivery.	**Good practice encourages active learning.** Learning is not a spectator sport. Students need to actively make what they learn part of themselves. **Good practice gives prompt feedback.** Students benefit from frequent opportunities to perform and receive suggestions for improvement. **Good practice emphasizes time on task.** Effective learning takes time; students need help in learning effective time management. **Good practice encourages cooperation among students.** Learning is enhanced when it is collaborative and social, not competitive and isolated.	**Course preparation and organization.** **Clarity and understandability.** **Quality of examinations.**
Knowledge. Excellent teachers are knowledgeable in their subject matter and in teaching strategies, enjoy learning, and engage in professional development to continually upgrade their knowledge.		**Knowledge of subject.**
Innovation. Excellent teachers integrate new ideas into their routines, search for new information and strategies, and are willing to take risks.		

Table 2. Comparative Typologies of Good Practice (Cont'd)

Roueche and Baker's Teaching for Success Model (1987)	Chickering and Gamson's Seven Principles of Good Practice (1987)	Feldman's Nine Exemplary Teaching Characteristics (1988)

Interpersonal Skills

Objectivity. Excellent teachers strive to be patient and understanding, evaluate objectively and fairly, and seek solutions, not blame.		**Overall fairness to students.** **Impartiality in evaluating students.**
Active Listening. Excellent teachers are committed to careful listening, paraphrase for clarification, and encouraging students to speak out.		
Rapport. Excellent teachers establish relationships with students through use of humor, showing personal interest in and respect for students.	**Good practice encourages student-faculty contact.** Frequent student-faculty contact in and out of classes is the most important factor in student motivation and involvement.	**Availability and helpfulness.**
Empathy. Excellent teachers model caring behavior, share personal experiences and feelings with students, and demonstrate understanding of others.		

Motivational Attributes

Commitment. Excellent teachers show heartfelt commitment to teaching and have high expectations for themselves and their students.	**Good practice communicates high expectations.** Expect more and you will get more. Expecting students to perform well becomes a self-fulfilling prophesy.	**Sensitivity to and concern with students' learning progress.**
Goal Orientation. Excellent teachers set personal goals and help students define and accomplish specific, realistic goals.		
Integrated Perception. Excellent teachers have a holistic view of both their students and their subject matter.		

Table 2. Comparative Typologies of Good Practice (Cont'd)

Roueche and Baker's Teaching for Success Model (1987)	Chickering and Gamson's Seven Principles of Good Practice (1987)	Feldman's Nine Exemplary Teaching Characteristics (1988)
Motivational Attributes		
Positive Action. Excellent teachers show enthusiasm and use a positive orientation to help students succeed. **Reward Orientation.** Excellent teachers are motivated by intrinsic rewards for teaching.		Enthusiasm for subject or for teaching.

Conclusion

When groups of educators gather to talk about teaching and learning, they typically turn to sharing stories—amazingly, remarkably similar stories—about their own experiences as students. Although they can only vaguely recall the good, the mediocre, and the poor, they can talk for hours on end about the excellent and the awful! Moreover, they can readily identify teaching characteristics at both ends of this spectrum; as well, they can describe the outcomes of these experiences—the exhilaration of the former and the mutilation of the latter.

As this chapter attests, there is much to be said and learned about extraordinary teaching—and, indeed, there has been much said and much more to be learned. Here, we have only scratched the surface of the findings from the last several decades of research and practice. And, not surprisingly, we returned to the beginning even as we ended this section: We may not agree wholeheartedly—and there is little reason to do so—on what makes for excellent teaching, but we appear to know it when we see it, or as in many cases, experience it. Teachers have enormous control over attitude and success—they literally carry the day! Our objective for this chapter was to provide a backdrop for what is to come—a collage of perspectives gleaned from award recipients who have been recognized for their sterling performance, who truly are in the best positions to teach us about excellence.

Chapter Five

Core Strategies for Effectively Teaching Content

I'm an addicted "door opener." So many students can only see the walls; others find the door but are afraid to knock or even touch the knob. I know I can oil the locks and coach students to open the doors. Not all will walk through, but the joy of following students as they launch themselves into new worlds is addictive, indeed.

—Barbara Clinton, Highline Community College (WA)

I n hope that the last chapter set the context with a bird's-eye view of research and practice that have directed and affected our thinking about what works in teaching and what teaching excellence is all about, we turn now to award recipients' perspectives as shared in their responses to our first survey question. Initially, many observed that they were intrigued by the idea of separating out the particulars of "teaching content" from "teaching students," and some commented that it was a good exercise for reminding them of the different mindsets and the instructional distinctions between "subject" and "affect." They cited examples whereby they would attempt to "blur the lines" between the two in their own classes, although they agreed that they generally tilted the behavior scales in favor of "affect." Although some of the particulars mentioned in the cluster of strategies for teaching content were equally at home conceptually, or at least a strong case could be made for it, in the other cluster of strategies for teaching students, by and large, the discussions produced a large number of amazingly crisp distinctions between the two. Analyzing the data was equally as interesting as the focus group activities, in particular, were in generating it.

Responses to "What Are the Core Strategies You Use to Be an Effective Teacher of Content?"

It has been said that excellent teachers love their students even more than they love the content of their courses or the particulars of their discipline. Working off that theory, we were drawn to the notion of separating our original, much larger question about core strategies for effective teaching into two parts, distinguishing between content and students or between subject and effect. Our first focus groups observed that we must get better at "building bridges" between what is to be learned and the learner, between the content and the student. In that regard, we asked two separate questions. The first addressed the teaching of content; the second addressed the teaching of students and will be discussed in chapter 6.

Know Your Subject

The first of the two most frequently mentioned core strategies for the effective teaching of content was "know your subject." That is, after all, where it all begins; it is the foundation on which one builds the interest for sharing and teaching. As individuals, these study participants were eager to stay current and keep abreast of changes in their fields and disciplines, to be on the cutting edge for their students.

Clearly, these participants understood and could demonstrate by their actions that knowing your subject is not a product, but a process. It is an ongoing, lifelong effort. Knowing one's subject has been identified as a critical characteristic of a superb teacher (Roueche & Baker, 1987; Wotruba & Wright, 1975). Knowing one's subject really well literally translates as remaining current enough to know you know!

Keep your intellect stimulated by reading, writing, and changing the content of the syllabus so that you stay fresh and current.

Know your subject and be prepared to explain it in two or three different ways, using examples, approaches, language, etc.—a valuable technique I learned during a high school teaching stint.

Know your material and be prepared to share it.

Know your subject and show that it is a vital part of your life.

Continue to study what you teach.

As a language teacher, I "steal" materials, techniques, and approaches from every available source—including my colleagues…Really!

Stay directly involved with your field of study.

Remain determined to never stop learning.

Practice what you preach—that is, work in the field that you are teaching.

Use a part of your summers to work on your discipline…great help…we should know what we want our students to know/master.

Know the content so thoroughly that you dream it!

Belong to several professional organizations. Magazines and meetings keep us on the cutting edge (of technology—I teach engineering).

Join professional, non-teaching organizations in order to remain current about what's really happening in the world the students will soon enter.

Solid knowledge of content area is a must; we can't teach what we don't really understand.

Remain a lifelong learner yourself.

Have fun making mistakes and realize that students know a thing or two.

Work as a team with colleagues to develop a consistent knowledge base.

Take post-graduate courses and take advantage of in-service opportunities.

Read, read, read—that helps keep us up to date on all the latest information on our subjects.

Deliver clear and passionate lectures; utilize appropriate support materials provided at workshops and conferences. Keep up with the latest research; conduct your own research and publish!

Emphasize Relevance, Application, and Utility

The second of the two most frequently mentioned strategies for the effective teaching of content was actually a cluster of related strategies: Emphasize relevance, application, and utility. Participants voiced literally thousands of examples of why and how content should be made useful and valuable to the learner. However, they first agreed that they had to know the students and their backgrounds before they could adequately create the links or expect them to do so. Undoubtedly, none of us would admit to loving or appreciating or enjoying all courses equally; today's students are no different in that regard. Interest usually originates in being an expert in a field of endeavor or being a novice that wants to become an expert. Few students, particularly those in general education courses or in introductory courses, are so committed to the pursuit of learning in that discipline or area that they will be highly motivated to learn. They may have great difficulty in seeing the relevance, or at least the same level of relevance, to their lives in every course they take.

Claire Weinstein, at The University of Texas, described the looks on her students' faces as she enters the room on the first day of her introductory statistics class—"expressions that range from apathy to hate, with a few smiles thrown in." She observed:

> I love statistics and think it is a crucially important and fascinating content area…how many of my students do you think share my feelings or motivational orientation? Very few. Most of the students in the class are not there because they want to become statisticians. They are there because taking statistics is required for a number of different majors.…What then are we to do as faculty to cope with this problem? (Weinstein, 1992, p. 1)

She also mentioned a number of strategies for helping students identify goals: brainstorming how the content could be of interest to them now and in the future; having students periodically write five-minute papers to discuss how the content is helping or could help a student meet other goals (personal or academic), relating content material to career types and choices, and helping students brainstorm their own futures. Most important, Weinstein advised that teachers should share their own excitement about the content and the subject, thus giving students a different perspective about the topic, the subject, and the field. Students have not always made up their minds about what their futures should look like—what interests they will pursue and what careers they will choose.

Try to find material for the students to read and write about that relates to exciting, controversial, and current topics.

Talk with individuals who have been involved actively with history—for example, legislators, military officers; have students do the same and report on their visits.

Show "real-life" examples of topics covered in class; make concepts clear, useful, and "sortable" to the student.

Relate content to students' life experiences.

Relate your own life experiences and situations to your content and share with students.

Show students that the content is interesting and exciting by being enthusiastic yourself.

Keep it simple and relevant—students want (and need) to see connections between content and how they can use or apply it.

Make applications relevant to students; frequently ask them to create examples together in groups to share with the class.

Make the world and subject relate to each other—not just to academics.

Show students how the concepts apply to "real-life" situations.

Have personal experience doing what you are teaching!

Have students relate the content to everyday global and local issues, and to their personal lives.

Begin learning about students' backgrounds and their learning styles during the very first class meeting.

Require hands-on experiences—such as conducting a political poll, beginning to end, rather than just reading about one in a history class.

Use the "Velcro technique"—connect what students already know to what they are about to be taught and should learn!

Think like a student. What would you want to know and how practical and application-oriented can it be?

Create hands-on experiences in labs and lectures.

Try to tie life skills to teaching principals.

Teach the "value" of discipline-specific knowledge that is absolutely necessary—for example, the importance of safe practice; but let the group guide you on how much "icing" they can absorb or tolerate.

Show/teach how the content is grounded in a real-world context—that is an important life skill, as well as an important college skill.

Bring the outside world into the classroom.

Use storytelling, especially if the story is related to personal experiences.

Integrate vocational and academic strategies, especially with team teaching.

Teach through story—we call these "paradigm cases" in nursing—that exemplify important concepts. This is a very vivid, engaging way to present content.

Take field trips, go on tours, attend conferences with the students; they really enjoy this effort!

Make any lecture material interesting and exciting. Make connections between content and students' lives. And get feedback to be certain that connections "click."

Be Organized

Research tells us that organized teachers draw students into the rules of the game, they make clear what they expect, and they state how students can meet their expectations. They give concise and sequential instructions and overviews of every step they will take throughout the course. Our participants were keenly aware that "putting it in writing, saying it precisely, referring to it frequently" were critical efforts to make toward helping students get their arms around what they were to do over the course of the term. Students could see the "what" and the "how"; as important, they were provided critical evidence that the teacher intended to help them be successful. Participants' third most frequently mentioned strategy was to be organized.

Be sure that content is broken down into understandable segments and presented sequentially!

Do the assignments over and over before giving them to the class.

Teach small topics, one at a time.

Start with the basic concepts and move to the more complex.

Present material in a structured, easy-to-follow format so that the students can relate the ideas and then use their inferencing skills to anticipate where the material is leading.

Have a handbook for each course.

Stick to the course outline.

During each class, review previously learned material, introduce new material, and apply new material.

Organize information carefully so that it is easier for students to learn.

Preview and review—over and over.

Establish a foundation—i.e., a common body of knowledge.

Review the objectives and write them in a bold, bullet format at the beginning of each class period.

Review the course syllabus regularly.

Review the series of elements covered so far often (in simplest terms, every meeting) and especially before moving to a new unit.

Clearly state the learning objectives. Relate academic objectives to practice.

Have definite goals. Have a clear and logical sequence of instruction.

Break down concepts into manageable, understandable parts.

Clump material into small units to improve students' chances to grasp it all.

Organize content within each class so that it flows logically from beginning to end.

Continually consult with colleagues in your content area for new ideas and innovation, better methods, and presentation formats.

Structure, structure, structure.

Content must be set within parameters, but be prepared to be flexible.

Handing out copies of all PowerPoint presentations encourages students to listen, rather than frantically copy.

Do not overload students with too many details; give content in small doses and build on them.

Make each new step (bite) small enough that students can "come with you."
Keep lessons in digestible, short units.

Break material down into sizable bites. Step-by-step procedures are best.

Take time each class to bring students back to where all of you are in the course.

Remember that they've been thinking of other things since your last class.

Never enter the classroom unprepared.

Provide a detailed syllabus and glossary to clarify the progress of the class related to subject areas the students will learn.

Don't change the rules of the system or the grading procedures in mid-stream.

I adapt my methods to the objectives of each course—e.g., some courses are very project-oriented, others geared toward research, others rely on group discussion, others use problem solving activities. There should be no pre-conceived notions here.

Tell them what you are going to cover, then cover it, and then review it.

Use the K.I.S.S. method—keep it short and simple.

Set High Expectations and Give Challenging Work

Our award recipients reported, in glowing terms, their expectations for all students. They were in teaching "for the long haul," many said; they had every intention of making a difference in students' lives. However, they talked openly of the wide range of impressions they could be making on students; they want the difference they make to be positive. Therefore, they agreed that it was absolutely mandatory that the expectations that they had for students would be set in a supportive environment that allowed for trying and retrying and failing and working toward improvement. Students had to learn that they were works in progress.

Two other interesting features regarding expectations came from the focus groups. First, there was widespread agreement that students watched their teachers carefully, not only for signs of acceptance, or of how well they were doing, but also for what they did and how they behaved, because they needed role models. In a study of Miami-Dade Community College's excellent faculty, Professor Thelma Altshuler illustrated this notion: "I take notes on the board as a demonstration of what [students] should do as they watch televised lectures" (cited in Roueche & Baker, 1987, p. 149). Second, there was great agreement that teachers could watch students carefully, too, by using "steering groups" to monitor how well or how poorly a lesson or an activity was developing. The students in these particular groups might change with the activity, but they were always there to help an instructor answer the critical questions: "Is anybody out there?" and "Are you with me?"

Finally, participants talked about making students responsible for their own learning—not leaving them alone out there but guiding them toward responsible behavior. Behavior is learned, and teaching responsible behavior, early on, is the teacher's responsibility. Then expecting, encouraging, supporting, and rewarding that behavior is critical to fostering independence and helping students develop skills with which to better learn for themselves.

All of these efforts coalesced into strategies that set high expectations and require challenging work.

Require library exercises and assignments and have students do research.

Pay strict attention to detail.

Explain the importance of doing homework; draw comparisons to sports—PRACTICE!

Expect students to have prepared for class.

Teach time consciousness and responsibility; put expectations in writing, discuss their importance, and then, for example, do not accept late work.

Have high expectations of your students, hold them to high standards, don't dumb down the course or let work slide; have high expectations of yourself and deliver the goods!

Strive to Foster Higher-Level Learning

High expectations correlate with higher-level learning. Respondents described their efforts to teach students how to learn—they paint the pictures and build the bridges. They do not assume that students can see the larger pictures or how ideas or issues fit together, and they do not assume that students know how to arrive at the place where that could occur. They implement learning-to-learn strategies.

For example, respondents talked about walking students through some useful procedures for reading their texts, accessing information from the Internet, and so forth. They discussed the importance of identifying priorities and the relative importance of content that is to be learned—students often believe that everything is of equal importance and advance toward cognitive overload quickly. Cognitivists warn that giving Monday's test again on Tuesday would be an eye-opening experience. Students who "forgot" on Tuesday what they had "known" on Monday's test did not actually learn the material; rather, they simply put it in short-term memory and then moved "new tenants, or information, into the rental space" (Weinstein, 2002, p. 1).

Faculty talked about encouraging higher-order thinking, teaching students to think with purpose, to develop cognitive structures by using techniques that facilitate creative thought. For example, faculty described designing questions that, as one participant offered: "would ratchet-up students' thinking," leading them to develop answers that would "teach them more than I ever could." Participants focus on strategies that foster higher-level learning.

Teach students how to learn and how to use what they learn in other classes, at home, and at work.

Help students discover relationships between content ideas/concepts.

Encourage discussion, using the Socratic method, to help students see the relevance of the context and the content to their lives.

Appreciate reaction and connection; let students know that you expect their input and will help them build bridges of information and relevance.

Facilitate learning—i.e., encourage students to think for themselves by letting them choose different paths, and demonstrate your confidence in their abilities to problem solve.

Help students see the patterns and concepts embedded in the content to promote conceptual learning.

Help students avoid memorizing anything! Help them make it a part of their thinking, and help them put together the larger picture of which facts or ideas are a part.

Have students explicitly describe how they will transfer content to their own lives and to other subjects.

Give challenging questions to groups that must arrive at a consensus and then give an oral presentation to the class.

Look at learning as a continuous interactive exchange—student to teacher and student to student.

Use simulations that require analysis, problem solving, and action.

Actively Involve Students

Students learn by doing—being active, not passive. The majority of strategies mentioned thus far have required activity, but these strategies are "going and doing" types. Participants described numerous strategies for getting students to speak up, speak out, move around, and physically be involved; they said they look for multiple ways to actively involve students.

Ask students to explain content in their own words.

Try to remember Gustave Flaubert's dictum: "The more you say, the less people remember." If students are to learn a language, they must speak!

Seldom give a direct answer. I'll ask questions until the student, or the class, comes to the answer.

Involve all of the senses as much as possible—movement, listening, touching, etc.

Students read and present examples from text to class.

"Trick" students into learning—plan a lesson that doesn't seem like a lesson, and then share your objective with them after the fact.

Have students keep a notebook throughout the semester. I enjoy seeing their entries, and it tells them a lot about their progress.

Have all students participate.

Use games to help students learn. One game that I call "Pass or Play" allows each student to attempt a response (become involved), and it helps me learn their names as we play.

Let students practice the material using different strategies and techniques: making small group presentations, creating posters, generating questions on content, writing a summary from memory, writing down what is not clear.

Get into teacher/student role exchanges.

Be flexible; let them have fun and do the teaching on occasion!

Embed the course content in rich, meaningful activities that allow students to discover their own meaning—apply the constructivist learning theory.

Involve students; ask them to give examples from their own lives, and give some from your life, as well. Recall will improve!

Use a Variety of Methods

Participants were full of great ideas for delivering content; their methods were illustrative of creative thinking and an unwillingness to become stale or boringly repetitious. They changed their delivery systems as much for their own benefit as for their students'. They talked about keeping the classroom "alive" and "lively." They described how they use a variety of methods. They alternate between lectures, discussion, audiovisual presentations, guest lecturers, field trips, computer applications, and the like. They were also willing to change directions at the drop of a hat, so to speak; they watched the sea of students' faces and their body language and let that feedback dictate their next steps. Finally, they noted that day and time of day the class is taught is an important consideration in their delivery style and pace.

Their strategies also included talking to colleagues about what "new" methods they were using that had been particularly successful. They read journals, took classes from colleagues and from others, and actively hunted for new techniques and equipment. Many observed that taking exciting "risks" on occasion was a trademark of their teaching styles. Ernest Boyer, former president of the Carnegie Institute for the Advancement of Learning, once observed that instructional risk takers are a rare phenomenon in today's college classrooms. The animated discussions around the use of multiple methods reminded us of an admonition heard years ago, but attributed only to an anonymous author: "If you have tried to do something and failed, you are vastly better off then if you tried to do nothing and succeeded."

Challenge yourself to periodically change your method of presentation; it keeps you "fresh."

Utilize resources, such as the library, peers, and the laboratory.

Be flexible.

Be repetitious; just teach the same point in many different ways.

Use different techniques and vary the methods of instruction according to the language students should read and their learning skills sets.

Teach for understanding, not for memorization and drill.

Use a variety of teaching methods; remember not everyone learns the same way.

Instead of lecturing on historical perspectives, have students create time lines of important events; go on field trips, use contemporary movies and music; have others, like lawyers, psychologists, and counselors to speak to the class. Keep things moving and exciting!

Teach content by providing the same information via multiple modalities.

Use or address the three learning modalities—audio, visual, kinesthetic—in every lesson.

Convey information in a variety of ways to maximize "hitting" the learning styles of all students.

Be able to explain a concept in a million different ways, if you must; hopefully, at least one will stick!

Be Student Centered

Responses were peppered with references to staying focused on how students could best respond to learning activities; they agree that they are student learning centered. Faculty saw students as individuals; they said it was "tough work" to do in a crowded classroom, but that "somebody had to do it." They considered individual differences to be strengths and believed that by helping individual students share the particulars of different learning styles, all students could grow stronger. Faculty agreed that it was their primary responsibility to meet students where they are and then *share* the responsibility for getting them where they need to go. But above all, their descriptions underscored their positive responses to the familiar Rousseau admonition: "In order to teach French to Johnny, you must first know Johnny."

Try to present every principle for each learning style.

Remind yourself that you continue to be a student of the larger learning environment.

Use comments and questions on journals to individualize instruction for each student.

Adjust the content of lesson plans to meet individual needs of each student. For example, lecture remains the same, but the lab experiences are adjusted to individual needs.

See each student as an individual—to see each student as "special," even sacred.

Use Humor

There is an amazing body of literature focused on the use of humor in teaching situations. Faculty in the focus groups observed that humor is a two-edged sword—it cuts both ways if used badly. It never works if it is used to make fun—unless it is making fun of oneself! They had numerous examples, using their own experiences as students to demonstrate the hilarious side of learning something for the first time or failing to get it time after time. Many explained that they could not even tell a joke, much less think of something really humorous in their own lives. Others indicated that they asked colleagues to share humorous exchanges or stories that they read or heard in other conversations; one said she believed she was just humor-deficient. The group laughed—she smiled broadly! But they agreed that they use humor however and whenever they can. Charles Schulz, the creator of "Peanuts" cartoon strips, observed: "Laughter is not just a pleasure. It's a necessity."

Non-derogatory humor works!

Humor makes a difference, but it must be used effectively.

Communicate Clearly

Faculty frequently mentioned the language they use in speaking with peers and colleagues and the efforts they make to tailor language to various situations with students. Experts talk a language of their own, when they are in groups, especially. Participants said that they chose their words carefully in the classroom, made eye contact often to see if "lights were on or off," and frequently asked if students were "with" them.

An interesting aside appeared during one discussion of this question regarding effective strategies for teaching content. A participant volunteered that she videotaped making introductory lectures before she gave them to her classes, especially if it was the first time that she had made that particular presentation. In viewing them later, she could frequently see gaps in her logic, or examples she had alluded to missing in action. And, others talked about how *hearing* themselves speaking before groups was a shocking experience, and they vowed to work harder on their enunciation and projection. They agreed that students need to have the teacher communicate clearly.

Speak clearly and loudly.

Use vocabulary with which students are familiar until they "get" the concept and then move on to the next level and weave in new terminology with the more familiar.

Learn their "language" and bring the material to them.

Unclear communication will kill you; being crystal clear up front is easier on everyone.

Be organized in your presentations; avoid jumping from topic to topic without getting closure before moving on.

Utilize Group Work and Collaborative Learning

Participants applauded the current interests in getting students more involved in their work by being involved with each other. They referred to their increasing emphasis on collaboration and group work—for written and oral assignments (in and out of class), fieldwork, and examinations, in particular. They supported the idea of collaboration over competition, and they agreed that the often-chaotic environment that simultaneous, multiple discussions could create was becoming the "sound of successful learning." Every focus group attended to the positive effects of using group work and collaborative learning.

Develop activities that require student interaction—effective ways to demonstrate the material to be learned.

Establish teams and partnerships.

Give several quizzes in a semester; students may work in small groups on them but turn in quizzes as individuals. They need not be bound to group consensus. They teach each other as they explain their rationales for answers.

Use group exams.

Use games—some can be designed by students for other students.

Have lots of student interaction and partnerships in producing course materials.

Have clear tasks laid out for all group work.

Use small group activities to encourage/enable high-level discussions.

Let students teach each other—if the students have achieved an appropriate learning level for the subject or the topic.

Collaborate with content-area instructors to make connections between content needs for success.

Put students into teams and have them develop instructional manuals for particular tasks that a specific job would require.

Give student 2–3 minutes to think about and discuss potential responses to questions with a partner.

Have students debate controversial topics in teams.

Affirm and Redirect as Necessary

Faculty observed that they must remain positive—whether in affirming students' good behaviors or redirecting bad behaviors. The key is keeping one's eye on the goal and helping students achieve it with more positive than negative experiences. Faculty reward behaviors and responses that they want to see; they create circumstances in which students have viable opportunities to be successful. Faculty agreed that affirming and redirecting as necessary are teaching skills that effectively recognize effort, encourage progress, and identify alternative paths to goals.

No matter what answer is offered during class discussion, I affirm it in some way; then I move on to another question that might "tease out" a better or a more appropriate or a more "correct" answer.

Immediate reinforcement of "acquired knowledge" is critical.

Affirm students' good behavior/answers; be sure to redirect their poor behavior/answers.

Use Technology to Its Fullest

Because two questions of the seven included on the survey focused on issues and problems associated with using information technology in instruction, survey respondents and focus session participants had ample opportunities to offer perspectives on the role of technology.

We direct readers to chapter 8 for a full treatment of using technology as an effective strategy for teaching content. However, as we observe in that chapter, faculty alluded to the fact that they are still climbing about the foothills in their use of information technology in instruction. There are higher mountains yet to climb, and they cannot yet visualize the full extent to which information technology can improve instruction, nor can they begin to imagine all that is possible. Therefore, although using technology to its fullest represented a small cluster of responses to this question, it is apparent that it also represented a major challenge to teachers of content.

Lecturers can be deadly without technology these days.

Make Use of Visuals and Provide Learning Resources

Faculty explained that students not only have diverse learning styles, but also those styles demand diverse ways to get to the material. Therefore, they are on the constant lookout for multiple ways to provide learning resources. Aware that many students do not have ample access to libraries, computers, or other sources of print materials, faculty create materials of their own and distribute to their classes. In this fashion, they can further expand their own role as a humane learning resource.

Use handouts.

Encourage the use of workbooks that accompany the text.

Pre-type outlines for students so that they do not have to spend all of their time just writing down information.

Use handouts of PowerPoint presentations of key points and reduce the amount of note taking. Students can pay attention and have key content available to them, regardless of their note-taking abilities.

Test and Assess Well

Faculty described multiple testing procedures. Many commented that they do not formally test anymore; they build tests into classroom activities that are evaluated and scores are combined as a major percentage of students' term grades. Collaboration, time-on-task, and application were common components in their descriptions of assessment strategies. Participants observed that the "proof of the pudding was in the eating," and they offered multiple strategies that could be implemented in the "tasting" stages of the learning experience. Many respondents recalled how painful formal tests had been for them as students and that they wanted to make assessment less traumatic and more accurate by eliminating as much of the "pain factor" as possible. They did not want students' negative feelings to skew test results; rather, they wanted to identify the best paths to assessing students' acquisition, understanding, and performance; they offered "test and assess well" as an effective strategy for learning about how effectively one has taught content.

Grade all written papers "pass" and "do again" so that students learn the process of rewriting (and I don't teach English).

Establish grades based on a variety of out-of-class assignments, not just formal testing.

Take-home tests are fine!

Pretest on content to be covered.

Test for understanding rather than only for facts.

Post a series of specific review questions.

Have old tests available as examples for your students.

Give homework quizzes and allow students to use any materials they have prepared in advance to answer the questions. This requires students to prepare better for class.

Offer review opportunities the day before testing occurs.

Create tests using various computer software packages.

Take-home comprehensive essay tests give students more time to consider their answers.

Require plenty of student-teacher office conferences.

Conduct Classroom Research

Finally, study participants looked to conducting classroom research as an effective tool for assessing their effectiveness as teachers of content, frequently describing combinations of strategies based on Cross and Angelo's Classroom Assessment Techniques. The Minute Paper and the Punctuated Lecture were mentioned frequently, but ultimately faculty were describing strategies for staying in touch—in a regular and timely fashion—with how well they were teaching and how well students were learning. Some participants referred to classroom assessment techniques, or classroom research, as critical "preventative measures," not unlike the worn message of "a stitch in time saves nine." The research they described took insignificant amounts of time; however, many faculty agreed that the results (critical feedback) justified that time and more!

Have students share "muddy" thoughts at the close of class.

Use the one-minute essay.

Have students answer two questions: What are the most important things you learned today, and what is still confusing you?

Classroom assessment techniques—including the Minute Paper, the muddiest point, focused listing, and one sentence summaries, to name a few—are all great!

Have students summarize and feed back sections of lectures.

Make explanations clear and continually check with students to make certain students thought so, too!

"Listen" to test results and student questions. Use frequent, brief student feedback techniques (CATs) to find out what students have "gotten."

Take opinion polls—agree/disagree—on answers that students bring in on their homework. Each side convinces the other to change their answers, based on process and reasoning.

Conclusion

> *Teaching isn't rocket science—it's* much *harder than that!*
> —A NISOD Excellence Award recipient

We concur! What we have learned is that teaching is a complex, complicated, oftentimes confusing, business. We are reminded of a critical first step toward becoming what we believe to be learning institutions. As Boyer observed: "If faculty and students do not see themselves as having important business to do together, prospects for effective learning are diminished" (1987, p. 141). These faculty saw themselves as having "important business to do," and they articulated the spirit of collaboration and courage that will be required to effect it.

In chapter 4, we included a wide range of issues and multiple research findings in a variety of disciplines and categories. We set that context for the equally wide variety and range of perspectives we gathered from these award recipients. Moreover, we observed that many of the clusters into which we sorted recipients' responses had their philosophical, conceptual, and virtual feet in both areas we were researching—core strategies for effectively teaching content and teaching students. Therefore, although we included discussions and comparative typologies of learning principles and excellent teaching practices in this overview, we did so to avoid artificially separating out many of the components that weave themselves through both camps. As a result, we dive quickly into participants' responses in the following chapter. The array of responses in every cluster or category we create speaks forcefully about the enormous power that all levels of the affective domain have in teaching and learning. We go forward "with feeling."

Chapter Six

Core Strategies for Effectively Teaching Students

Creative teaching brings together style and imagination in a process not unlike painting or sculpturing.…It is an art.

—Kelley and Wilbur (1970, p. 137)

F ew of us who viewed the movie, *The Paper Chase,* will ever forget the scene in which the law professor throws out a question to his class and then calls on a male student—even though the student's hand was not in the air—for an answer. After the student pulls himself together and gives his answer, the professor reaches into his pocket, pulls out a coin, offers it to the young man, and advises him to "call your mother and tell her that you will never be a lawyer." Of course, as the director had hoped, laughter immediately erupted from the audience! The professor's directive was, in fact, artfully timed, craftily droll, and overwhelmingly unexpected—in sum, a performance to be remembered.

Why is this scene so clear and sharp in our memories? We suspect that it released a flood of flashbacks—perhaps none quite so traumatic but painful nonetheless. Mixed together were the student's fears of being called on when unprepared to answer, ridiculed for a poor response, bullied by someone "in charge," and separated from any possibility of support or comfort from classmates. And, ultimately, these fears were mixed with the joy of not being in that student's shoes! Unfortunately, it was likely that the majority of school-age children and adults in that audience could have contributed to a lively discussion if the movie had ended with that scene. In our vernacular, that scene was and would have been a "teachable moment."

It would have been a teachable moment because it is a stellar case study in *affect*; it is all about feelings! And it is about performance! More than 25 years ago, after Kelley and Wilbur concluded their major study of successful teaching, they observed that when all is said and done, teaching is an *art*. They and we agree with numerous other researchers of teaching excellence that teaching is done best when performed by talented and committed artists. In the previous chapter, traits of good practice that we drew from the literature included six that Kelley and Wilbur (1970) listed in their top 10 (despite its age, this landmark investigation still holds true for today's teachers); the other four traits or characteristics that they identified were enthusiasm, personal interest in students, charisma, and character.

To these, we added some characteristics from Eble's extensive list that included generosity, honesty, reserving judgment, and willingness to take risks. We were faced with the enormous task of separating out the human, affective part of teaching from the instructional design, or practice, part. It would have been an artificial separation any way we tackled it; therefore, we took a more logical approach and let the lines blur as they may. Clearly, in the classroom, the talent lies in the subtle meshing of behaviors from the cognitive and the affective domains; here we attempt to tease out some of what we know and some of what these award recipients confirmed from the "feeling" dimension of teaching.

Responses to "What Are the Core Strategies You Use to Be an Effective Teacher of Students?"

Show Respect

The most frequently mentioned strategy for teaching students laid the foundation on which to build positive relationships in the classroom; respondents observed that their first responsibility was to show respect. Every focus group initiated a major discussion about the diversity that students bring to the classroom. One participant indicated that she was amazed that the majority of her students could get everything done that they had to do, just given the overwhelming combination of family, job, and academic responsibilities. She continued that she was surprised they could maintain their energy and keep so many balls in the air throughout an entire term. Others indicated that they were not just surprised that students could complete one term and then another, but rather that students with "so much on their plates" ever chose to come to college at all. They respected their spunk and applauded their decisions; they respected them for their choices and their efforts. Yet, faculty agreed that although it was their job to help students learn to balance these responsibilities and stay focused—and when necessary to make allowances for unexpected and unavoidable circumstances that affected students' performance—it was not their job to expect less of them.

"Integrated perception" is a common term for this view of the whole student as an individual with a life outside of the classroom (Roueche & Baker, 1987, p. 152)—a strong characteristic identified in other studies of excellent teachers (e.g., Brown & Thornton, 1963; Miller, 1972). Faculty who teach from the perspective that students have a "real life" outside of the classroom observe that over time they become more adept at integrating subject matter with students' needs and life experiences and helping them draw out the relevance of course content to their lives. Faculty indicated that, ultimately, they improved their students' and their own worldviews.

Respect all students—yes, even the most "difficult" ones. Never play favorites.

Always treat students as important human beings.

Keep announced office hours.

Answer questions as best you can. If you can't, direct students to a resource for an answer and ask them to report back.

Don't surprise students by changing directions in midstream. Be consistent.

Be realistic.

Listen and relate the material based on their viewpoints.

Remember that this is unfamiliar territory to students.

Your role is to facilitate their learning, not to impress them with yours.

Respect students as much as you expect them to respect you.

Do not contrast or compare students in the classroom or out of it.

On the first day of class, tell students that learning is like rowing a boat; together; we are in the same boat and rowing in the same direction. Let them know that we are all part of a team, that we're in this together, and that we should be headed toward success.

Always be honest with students about their progress.

The Socratic method is useful in going from the known to the unknown. [I'm retiring; one student wrote: "It's sad that future students will never have their brains picked by you."]

A "dressing down" session with a student is permissible if his/her behaviors have been irresponsible or questionable. However, always begin and end the session with positive statements and express your confidence in the talents and opportunities to choose more appropriate behaviors in the future. Then comment on improvement as you see it happen.

Listen to students and CARE.

Seek eye contact; expect to get it back; you will, eventually.

Stress the importance of students' talents and experiences.

Treat students as you would wish to be treated.

Maybe it's the terminology, but if you're not "teaching students," you're not teaching.

Make the classroom a safe place for every student to practice expressing personal truths and experiencing respect for those truths.

Assume right away that each student is capable of good work and will demonstrate that during the term.

Help students find their "passion" for life; it leads to learning.

Be Enthusiastic and Share Joy

The second most frequently discussed strategy was the combination of being enthusiastic and sharing joy. In *Education and Ecstasy,* Leonard (1969) set out to describe what he referred to as "education's most powerful ally"—the sheer joy of learning; one participant told us that someone once accused her of being "addicted to joy." Our participants consistently used terms such as "passion" and "excitement." All in all, they were aware of the contagious nature of their enthusiasm for their subject and their students. Most of all, we heard the participants warning against, at all costs, sharing their own problems with students, that their job was to be enthusiastic about their mission and joyful about their tasks.

> *If you have not slept, or if you have slept, or if you have headache, or sciatica, or leprosy, or thunder-stroke, I beseech you, by all angels, to hold your peace, and not pollute the morning.*
> —Ralph Waldo Emerson

Show enthusiasm for the subject.

Share your glee at being with them and your excitement about the importance of the topic. It works!

It's true that you can lead a horse to water and that you can't make him drink. But, you can paint pictures of a cool, refreshing, inviting liquid and make him thirsty.

Students need to know that you LOVE what you're doing and that you are excited about helping them learn.

Smile; it's contagious.

Demonstrate Care and Empathy

Faculty in the focus groups underscored the importance of creating a "caring climate" in their classrooms—making classrooms comfortable places where students felt at ease to share ideas and establish relationships with classmates and with them. Some suggested that although comfortable physical surroundings could not always be achieved in a college's "institutional" setting, they tried, nonetheless, to create the comfortable feeling they effected in the living rooms of their own homes. One participant offered that she had been in far too many classrooms that could more aptly be labeled "existing rooms," a term she borrowed from interior decorator Lucy Throop, who in 1910 disparaged the creation of cold and sterile "living-rooms."

Discussions focused on being empathetic toward students—walking in their shoes, putting themselves in their students' places, and trying to "understand reality from another's perspective" (Roueche & Baker, 1987, p. 166). Defined as a highly developed ability to recognize, interpret, and act on the "clues" that others give, "active empathy" (Klemp, 1977) was high on participants' affective lists; they credited their ability to demonstrate care and empathy with creating climates for successful teaching and improved learning. In particular, faculty observed that they depend on such strategies as sharing the secrets of their own successes and their failures to help students better deal with their own awkward or difficult situations.

You cannot teach someone who is too uncomfortable to learn; create a comfortable learning environment.

See students as learners and future professionals. Allow them to contribute. Encourage creativity.

Be available outside of class for help and/or discussion.

Show you LIKE them.

Take a personal interest in every student.

Listen to students, their concerns and questions.

Care about students as individuals.

Show them that you care.

Each student is important; your caring can be the turning point in an education and a life.

Let students know early on that you are "there" for them, that they are your primary interest.

They don't care how much you know IF they don't know how much you care.

Remind yourself that you were once where they are now.

Remember that we are all in the process of being learners and students, simultaneously.

Try to connect with students as individuals through written, personal responses to essays.

Understand the outside influences that affect students' academic performances.

Express *genuine* concern; insincerity is obvious!

Remember that you are not just the "speaker up front." Be seen as a model and mentor; say the appropriate things, project a positive attitude, and support your values.

Demonstrate respect for diversity and each student's feelings of self-worth.

Love them.

Stimulate interest, thinking, learning…in that order.

Be nice, friendly, kind, fair, and firm.

Talk to students in your office—the "old rocking chair" techniques work to get them to open up and share.

Let students see your human side; relate real applications from your own experiences to course content.

Share your own life's stories.

Share your own struggles and successes in the subject you are teaching.

Many students are first-generation college-goers and/or they are older and more mature than the more traditional students; they need you to be their cheerleader. Share "you."

Hold to High Expectations

Respondents identified the strategy of holding high expectations of their students as critical to making a difference in students' lives; some referred to the potential of the "Pygmalion effect"—a powerful motivator that has been found to encourage students to believe in and outperform themselves. They warned, however, that pairing high expectations with high standards could test the resolve of insecure students or those more academically unprepared; pairing expectations and standards at high levels, particularly with these students, will be successful in only the most supportive climates for learning.

Self-satisfaction is an anticipated outcome for students who strive to meet high expectations. Many faculty reported that students told them they had not wanted to "let them down," and so they worked harder to achieve the goals established in that teacher–student relationship. And, faculty continually returned to the notion that they had the obligation and responsibility to help students develop the tools and the skills important to reaching the levels that high expectations required. They encouraged students to adopt improved organizational skills, good study habits, and the like. Essentially, holding to high expectations provided a strong base for developing good relationships with their students and providing them with a good role model for improved learning.

> Raise the levels of expectation, and don't pander to mediocrity. If you expect more, you will get more. If you expect less, you may find that students will give you what you want!

> Encourage student-parents to model good study habits for their children.

> Challenge students to achieve higher levels of learning.

> Have high expectations.

> Articulate your expectations of students; let them know that you recognize their strengths and capabilities as human beings. Believe in students even before they believe in themselves. Share that belief with them.

> Be a cheerleader! Let students know that you expect them to learn and pass the course!

> Constantly challenge your students.

> Remind students that the grade they "get" is the grade they "earn."

> Challenge students' preconceptions and biases.

Encourage personal responsibility and independent thinking.

Require—yes, *require*—students to remain open to new ideas and different personalities.

Walk Your Talk

"Talk is cheap," our respondents observed; they agreed that walking the talk was a pathway to student trust and respect. A teacher's responsibility, in the words of one participant, was comedian Flip Wilson's admonition: "Write no checks with your mouth that your body can't cash." Other respondents observed that consistency is critical, always doing what you say you will do. Moreover, as another focus group participant suggested, doing what you say you will do is even more powerful when it is done earlier rather than later—at least, in a timely manner. Apparently, there is a useful corollary to the "walk the talk" rule—"timing is everything."

Believe in the importance of your subject matter. Be a role model: demonstrate the skills you want students to develop.

Be available—match your students' energy! They work hard—you work hard. If they don't, make the "trough of learning" very inviting. Make them feel *seriously* invited to the learning party!

Being "real" translates to being on the same "human level" as students; they tell me that's important.

Constant reinforcement is important; the students are responsible for their learning, but you for their support.

Never, ever lie to students.

Be your "word." Honor your contracts. Hold yourself accountable to collecting and returning work as assigned.

Always arrive on time and prepared. Don't expect students to demonstrate interest if you don't demonstrate it yourself.

Foster Student Motivation and Success Skills

Another core strategy focused on helping students find their own ways to improved performance. Faculty emphasized the need to help students identify what might work for them; help them visualize being successful. They indicated that they saw enormous returns for fostering student motivation, learning, and life success skills.

Teach students study techniques and good student habits; check on their techniques.

Design learning-activity assignments which engage the students in moving from reading to responding to sharing their thinking.

Praise failures when they can be useful pathways to learning.

Teach from the heart.

Say, "look at me—nothing special. I can succeed; so can you."

Try your very best to "catch" students doing *anything* correctly; then PRAISE them.

Wear appropriate clothing. Students deserve a "professional" image. Many students come from cultures where clothes really matter.

Have students who have performed well on an exam or in a presentation share their strategies with their classmates. Soon, others will want to do the same.

Make Contact

We were reminded of the importance of making contact with students—not only by being there for them as a teacher, but by creating communities and relationships that they can count on to provide support, encouragement, and help. Creating situations in and out of the classroom that will foster the development of networks and "hot lines" will help establish relationships that can be important beyond the classroom walls and long after the course has been completed. Participants observed that human interaction makes education more "humane."

Make certain that students get to know each other. Encourage them to help and support each other in class.

Having to present content to students who demonstrate a variety of learning styles and diverse backgrounds requires that you have ample information about both, in writing, at the beginning of the term.

Smile when you enter the classroom! Always greet students as if you're happy to be there; show them how much fun this experience can be.

Attend students' events: basketball, football, plays, honor society meetings, student senate and other organizations, etc.

Tell stories about yourself to enliven the lessons.

Promote student feedback and listen: Students are a lot like icebergs—there is a lot below the surface.

Speak to each student everyday; call each by name and sometimes refer to something personal about them.

Establish a human bond with students.

Learn their names, early.

Spend time with your students, get to know them, and do something with them outside of class.

Be available.

Teachers should work at a "no walls" approach to teaching.

Schedule time for "voluntarily mandatory conferences." Meet students one-on-one and in small groups (but recommend no more than four in a group).

Invite students to your home as a group—perhaps at Christmastime or after graduation ceremonies.

Take students to career-oriented conferences, arrange for their housing, etc.

The team concept is "in." Form teams for labs. Allow a team to "fire" unproductive members. If the unproductive students join another group and get fired again, they must complete the work on their own. Welcome to the real world!

Support student comments verbally and with body language.

Peer-teaching is a valuable teaching strategy.

Encourage students to interact with each other; focus on cooperative work and less on competition. Two (or more) minds are always better than one.

Encourage students to support each other and encourage a useful amount of interdependence.

View teaching as a battle for the students' hearts and minds—without the heart, the mind could care less.

Work on students' attitudes from the second they walk into class.

Pick out the wallflower student, or the introvert, and work up the list!

Be available 24/7, by online connection at home and in the office.

Try to help any student who comes forward for it. (I give students my home phone number.)

Tell stories about yourself; become human.

Don't stop teaching as you exit the classroom door.

Recognize that your time in the classroom is only a small part of what you do as a teacher.

Establish a relaxed classroom atmosphere in which students can be comfortable and be themselves.

Give students your e-mail address. [Another participant responded: Me, too; I wish I had one!]

Keep honing your interpersonal skills of reflexive listening, openness, using humor to reduce frustrations.

Make each class feel that it is special.

Set the tone for the class during the very first class meeting; get students to RELAX about being there and about the subject, as best you can.

Be a friend!

Share your mistakes with no embarrassment. Guess what? We're not perfect!

Check frequently with students to learn what they think you are doing that helps them the most, or what is distracting, dull, and turning them off.

Schedule appointments with every student at least twice during each term to ask, specifically—What is working for you? What is not? How can I help you learn better?

Have students learn each other's names the first week, as you learn them.

Listen to Students

Making contact with students requires asking questions of them—and then listening to their responses. Henry David Thoreau observed: "The greatest compliment that was ever paid me was when one asked me what I thought, and attended my answer." Earl Koile, an emeritus professor at The University of Texas, has conducted numerous studies about listening and reported, regrettably, that the two professional groups most often identified as "nonlisteners" were medicine and education! His findings included accusations that physicians and teachers were too quick to answer their own questions, were not willing to wait an appropriate and useful amount of time to allow the intended respondent to formulate an answer, and were frequently guilty of ignoring or misinterpreting questions or comments by their patients or students and pressing on apparently unaware that they were acting on inaccurate information. We observed that the excellent teachers involved in this current study contribute significantly to changing the reputation educators apparently have earned!

Many of the responses that logically could have been included in this category found their way into others, particularly the category we titled "making contact." Mindful, active listening bubbled up in every focus group as an enormously important strategy, a major teaching "skill," and a basic ingredient for effective interaction. Participants discussed the need to repeat student responses or comments, to paraphrase them—as much to assure themselves that they understood correctly as to emphasize the value of student contributions. Research tells us that paraphrasing for clarification, taking time to hear students out, and being willing to listen out of class, as well, are among the more common behaviors exhibited by faculty who are attentive and active listeners. Excellent teachers appear to work hard at being excellent listeners.

> Talk with students wherever you see them; take time to let students know how interested you are in them; actively listen to what they are saying.

> Above all else, be a good listener!

Encourage Humor and Humanity

Respondents told us that their sense of humor makes them more "human" to their students, increases the likelihood that students see them as more accessible, and helps students accept better the subject they are teaching. The literature tells us that there are no proven links between student learning and fun, but we suspect that there are any number of potential links between doing something that is fun and enjoyable, and something that must and should be done. They use humor and encourage humanity.

> Use humor often and in ways that relieve stress or break up a too-long presentation; find ways to use humor to dismiss a bad idea or attitude and help avoid either becoming a personal attack.

> Sing to students in class! [One focus group participant responded: "I promised them I wouldn't."]

> Sometimes it is useful to "look" foolish in order to make a point.

> Have fun!

Humor is an important teaching strategy; it helps keep the classroom "light" and nonthreatening; it goes a long way toward helping students feel "at home."

Demonstrate that you care about students by sharing your humor with them.

Make learning fun!

Use cartoons in presentations; embed jokes in your handouts.

Bring humorous real stories, relevant to the situation, into your teaching.

Maintain a sense of humor, especially about yourself.

Find ways to laugh at your mistakes!!

Poke fun at yourself—at least until students laugh!

Encourage students to open up and disagree with each other and with you.

Be Flexible

A country-western song extols the virtues of being like a tree that will bend in the wind but not break. Critics tell us that educators are inflexible, that they cannot break out of old habits, that their feet are firmly planted in tradition, and that they are unbearably resistant to change. Our participants observed that they are at their best when they are being risk takers. They appreciate the opportunities to be flexible, and they encourage their students to do the same.

Take risks! In "The Dance," vocalist Garth Brooks reminds us that we should experience *all* of life, that even when we know how it all will end, we shouldn't miss the "dance." Don't let your students sit out the "dance"—draw them into it!

Be creative; take chances with your approaches to teaching and encourage students to be creative in their approaches to their assignments.

Try more than one way to get the message across—*something* will work. And, maybe all of them will!

Praise, Celebrate, and Reward Students

Several years ago, a community college president, addressing an audience of other presidents and administrators, observed that she had learned a great deal about administration from attending dog obedience classes with her "four-legged children." She indicated that perhaps the most useful lesson she learned was to be effusive with praise whenever the dogs responded well to commands or situations. She admitted that the trainer's directive, "praise him, praise him," was equally as effective with humans as it was with dogs. She strongly recommended it to others as an effective tool with which to encourage and support responsible and appropriate behaviors. Praise was the celebration of good deeds!

The history of educational institutions reminds us that universities were established, originally, around celebration, primarily of the arts—music, art, drama. As universities turned their interests toward training, for example, many of the celebratory features of their missions disappeared or, at least, were diminished or overshadowed by others. Many of these institutions lost their focus, and many lost much of their life's blood. These award recipients spoke with passion about the critical need to praise, celebrate, and reward students.

Reward and acknowledge—good thinking on our parts!

Praise students; encourage them. Make a list of 100 encouraging phrases and keep it handy.

Write brief notes on their papers—comment on improvements they have made and give them encouragement when they need it.

Feed 'em, hug 'em (when allowed), call 'em, and tell 'em they can do it!

Celebrate milestones!!

Conclusion

Some college teachers simply do not age. Their work, if anything, becomes more vibrant and youthful as they mature. How do they sustain their vitality throughout a long career in teaching? What keeps them motivated? These questions have intrigued researchers for nearly a century.
—Walker and Quinn (1996, p. 315)

As we closed out this chapter, we agreed that we were able to once again confirm so many notions we had long held about teachers, in general—the first being that if you are not a good human being or if you are not humane, teaching will not make you either one or the other. Teaching is a high-risk human enterprise; you must *be one* going in to survive it yourself and to give students any chance of surviving along with you! The second is that chances are good that you would not be drawn to it, otherwise.

These award recipients reminded us that teaching is a two-way street and all about feelings. It is a "shared journey" that can only be enjoyed when taken with verve and excitement—with the full range of emotions. These faculty talked about love of subject and love of students; about passion and holding students in high regard; they spoke to the importance of doing something that helped them "make a difference"—not only for the number and magnitude of the personal and professional rewards for themselves, but for the rewards they could offer others. Many spoke to the "selfishness" that their profession allowed them; they had the opportunities to try new things and to take risks that those in other professions were not allowed. We suspect that an enormous wealth of information is just beyond the threshold of future research about risk-taking behavior. We were not left to wonder whether they believed that they had the best jobs in the world; rather, it was obvious that the intrinsic rewards they enjoyed fueled the flames of their professional fires.

We end this chapter with a story, another true and compelling one. It speaks to celebration—simultaneously, a motivator, an acknowledgment of appreciation, and a gift of surprise. Several years ago, we decided to pay special attention to celebrations. One idea we had was that a standing ovation was a rare event indeed and few in our world had experienced it. We decided to have a standing ovation for no apparent reason and see what might develop! So, at an after-NISOD conference party several years ago, those of us who had already arrived agreed that when the next person or persons came through the door, we would stand and give them thunderous applause for several minutes—an actual standing ovation.

As it was, the next person to arrive was a junior secretary, who had very recently joined our staff and brought along her husband to meet the group. They entered the room; we all stood and applauded for almost two minutes although they looked surprised, then pleased, then embarrassed. When the applause died down, she said, "So, how did you all find out that I'm pregnant?" It was a surprise to all of us, for sure. One never knows exactly where celebration might lead, but we contend that it is always worth the effort to find out.

This is all to say that celebrations are acts of recognizing and applauding life's good things. Our participants observed that too many of their students had far too few celebrations in their lives. These faculty were committed to celebrating the days of their own and their students' lives—as effective teachers of students.

Chapter Seven

Assessing Learning:
How We Know They Know

The way to gain a good reputation is to endeavor to be what you desire to appear.

—Socrates

"The ultimate test of institutional effectiveness is assessing what and how much our students are learning. What value do we add to students from their point of entry until they exit…?" Answering the critical question, "What and how much are your students learning?" presents "an unparalleled opportunity—and we should gladly meet the task" (Hudgins & Williams, 1997, pp. 63, 53). The value-added question will be answered essentially by the quality of the teaching and learning occurring in the institution.

We begin with a brief review of recent developments in college initiatives regarding institutional effectiveness, to provide a broader context in which to couch the perspectives of the award recipients. Following this overview, we turn to the responses from the teaching professionals who are on the cutting edges of student learning assessment practices.

The Centrality of Learning and Institutional Effectiveness

There is widespread agreement that college administrators and faculty can no longer dodge, ignore, or poorly respond to questions from stakeholders about what and how well students are learning; colleges that claim they do not know or cannot measure the outcomes of a student's time with them raise serious questions about their quality and effectiveness. The growing body of research and documentation regarding institutional effectiveness practices, measures, and mandates tells us that the current demands by all stakeholders for improved learning and student performance are not going away, but rather they will become more intense and intrusive unless colleges decide to measure and demonstrate their effectiveness:

> …colleges should want to make sure that students are learning…When taken seriously, assessment shapes curricula and instructional practice. The business community axiom that "what gets measured, gets done" holds true in education as well.

> In…a culture of evidence—assessment is a necessary and integral part of greater student achievement. It becomes predominantly a tool for improvement: to improve learning, teaching, and the curriculum. Learning-centered assessment can be linked to courses and allow professors to answer for themselves the important questions of what, how much, and how well their students are learning. (AACU, 2002, pp. 39–40)

Colleges are implementing strategies to measure their effectiveness, relevancy, and responsiveness to all stakeholders, but few have successfully matched their outcomes to their mission statements (Roueche et al., 1997). That is, they do not measure the appropriate outcomes that would tell them if, indeed, they are achieving their missions. However, there are increasing numbers of colleges whose experiences prove that serious engagement in measuring effectiveness and moving through and beyond the questions of how best to select and design strategies for measuring learning and what to measure, pays off. The lessons they have learned and the strategies they have employed could be useful examples for others.

In that regard, we offer overviews of strategies being implemented by two colleges whose efforts and successes we have observed over the last decade. Their experiences indicate that colleges can improve their performance by using institutional data to bring about appropriate change. The common elements in the effectiveness strategies being implemented at these colleges include the practices of (1) creating and monitoring annual activity plans in which support is tied to institutional priorities and (2) benchmarking their achievements against mandated criteria and the achievements of exemplary performers.

Midlands Technical College

In a state that ties 100 percent of its funding for higher education to performance, Midlands Technical College (MTC), in South Carolina, has more than a decade of effort and data driving their effectiveness measures. Each spring, every department and unit of the college develops action strategies for the coming year; these plans are reviewed to ensure that they match up well with college goals and priorities. They identify action strategies, develop an annual budget, and allocate resources.

MTC's Assessment Activities Plan identifies college-wide action strategies, identifies the dates when major planning and assessment activities will occur, lists the standards for the indicators of effectiveness, and delineates the externally mandated assessment reports that are to be completed during the year. The plan is considered the road map for the year's activities.

MTC's Report Card is an annual update that describes current data on assessment activities and effectiveness standards. Used within the college to recognize success and to plan for upcoming resource allocation, MTC's Community Report is also mailed to the community-at-large. Data available in these reports also help identify outstanding employees and programs and lead to their recognition by college administrators and trustees.

MTC uses a set of benchmarks, known as critical success factors, to measure its progress:

- accessible, comprehensive programs of high quality
- student satisfaction and retention
- post-education satisfaction and success
- economic development and community involvement
- sound, effective resource management
- dynamic organizational involvement and development

Each of these six critical success factors was described further by indicators of effectiveness that were to be measured against corresponding sets of criteria or standards; sources for the standards were national and regional criteria, accreditation standards, national competency exams, and empirical institutional data. The indicators were crafted from the institution's responses to these two questions: "What do we want the results of effectiveness to be?" and "What specific evidence are we willing to accept that the results have been achieved?" (Hudgins & Williams, 1997, p. 60)

The ultimate goal of these effectiveness strategies is to exceed the state legislature's criteria in its accountability mandates and the criteria of the regional accrediting agency. Among the lessons MTC described as having learned during the effectiveness effort is that faculty participation is critical. Unfortunately, many educational accountability and total quality management programs focus on administrative procedures. To accomplish positive change in student learning and success, faculty must assume leadership roles and become active participants in classroom research (Hudgins & Williams, 1997, p. 65).

Community College of Denver

The Community College of Denver (CCD), in Colorado, has for more than a decade strived to keep excellent teaching and learning at the top of its institutional agenda. Its annual planning cycle involves every individual and every unit of the college. This cycle is tended carefully, as it monitors institutional achievements and effectiveness outcome data and guides appropriate changes that data indicate should be made within the institution. Included in CCD's vision statements over this last decade are the goals of "providing state-of-the-art learning, teaching, and working opportunities…[and achieving comparably high] success rates of students of all races, classes, and cultures" (McClenney, 1997, p. 74).

One strategy for providing state-of-the-art opportunities has been CCD's efforts to learn from others.

> An institution seeking quality and access must place its assessment and clarification processes against those of other institutions that are comparable, competitive, or potential role models. These other institutions can serve as measuring sticks or benchmarks against which to assess the potential and actual achievement of one's own institution. Such comparisons permit distinctions to be drawn so that the unique quality of one's own institution can be more readily identified and nurtured. (Bergquist, 1995, p. 258)

The college decided to benchmark its programs and strategies against designs and data from other colleges recognized for specific best practices. Small teams of CCD administrators, faculty, and directors visited these selected colleges and reported what they learned. In particular, they focused on how CCD could use what they had learned. They organized the data and descriptions they collected into three categories: "(1) designing and implementing responsible change; (2) showing a program or strategy is headed in the right direction; and (3) predicting which CCD practices have the greatest likelihood for continuing success" (Roueche et al., 2001, p. 84).

The goals achieved at CCD, the most diverse institution of higher education in the state, would be extraordinary in any study, but they are particularly noteworthy in a study of teaching excellence. Current data show that comparable graduation and success rates have been achieved for all students, regardless of race or academic preparation upon matriculation at CCD. These data and others documenting the college's progress and achievements are shared with stakeholders in and out of the institution in CCD's annual Accountability Report, Achievements/Results, and Annual Report. Reports of student satisfaction and success are included in the course catalog and college handbook.

The college has identified the significant milestones to creating its vision and creating its climate for success as follows:

- exit competencies specified for all programs
- assessments developed for all competencies
- assessments incorporated into regular program reviews

- Teaching/Learning Center developed
- development and integration of six critical skills across the curriculum (reading, computation, writing, computing, speaking/listening, and diversity)
- development of values for teaching and learning
- professional development program to reinforce the teaching values
- classroom observation instruments and student evaluation of instruction modified to reflect values
- faculty merit pay plan developed with 80 percent of pay based on measured teaching effectiveness (Roueche et al., 2001, p. 102)

The former president of CCD, Byron McClenney, observed of his faculty:

> They have been involved for a decade in determining the standards against which…measurements can be made. Faculty routinely make clear to students what they should know and be able to do as they exit courses and programs, and they routinely plan for new interventions to help more students be successful. (Roueche et al., 1997, p. 78)

Some of What We Know About Methods of Evaluating Teaching

Historically, four groups have been involved in measuring teaching effectiveness: teachers, students, external judges, and educational researchers (Alfred, 1994). The accuracy of teaching evaluations from each of these groups has been reviewed extensively, and the perspectives each of them bring to evaluation offer valid and useful insights into what constitutes good teaching. Although faculty self-assessments are included as important to both identifying and promoting teaching effectiveness (Angelo, 1996; Arreola, 1995; Svinicki et al., 1996), most current researchers agree that teaching effectiveness is best assessed through triangulated sources: "Experts on faculty assessment and evaluation agree that we need teaching assessment data from at least three different sources: from the instructors themselves, their students, and their faculty peers and colleagues" (Angelo, 1996, p. 61).

Self-Evaluation

Self-evaluation and self-reflection are increasingly promoted as useful tools in assessing and improving teaching effectiveness. Faculty's self-assessments offer data most closely related to the individual faculty member's personal values and goals (Arreola, 1995). Nevertheless, a number of researchers point out challenges with self-evaluations of teaching effectiveness: Most teachers tend to assess themselves positively, and many do not know how to assess their own performance accurately (Seldin, 1988); faculty self-evaluation has a very low correlation with colleagues' and administrators' ratings (Arreola, 1995; Centra, 1996). However, there is significant evidence that faculty self-evaluations correlate positively with students' *overall* ratings and that faculty most likely to improve in response to feedback from students are those whose student ratings are less positive than their self-evaluations (Paulsen & Feldman, 1995).

Evaluations by Students

Perceptions of college students reported by way of formal student ratings are the most common source of information in higher education about effective teaching (Arreola, 1995; Cross, 1994). Use of student ratings in a wide range of public and private institutions has increased over the last two decades from 80 percent (of 756 institutions surveyed) in 1976 to 95 percent (of 630 institutions surveyed) in 1985 (Paulsen & Feldman, 1995). The tendency for institutions to rely on student evaluations as the sole or predominant source of faculty assessment data has led to a common perception of faculty evaluation as synonymous with student ratings of instructors (Arreola, 1995).

Notwithstanding their widespread use, student ratings remain controversial and greatly misunderstood. To answer the perennial question—"How well can students evaluate the effectiveness of teaching?"—every reasonable factor that could bias student ratings has been studied "almost to the point of exhaustion" (Cross, 1994, p. 690). For the most part, this research has shown student ratings to be reliable and objective. Nevertheless, a number of common myths continue to circulate about inadequacies of student ratings despite consistent empirical evidence to the contrary (Aleamoni, 1987; Feldman, 1996):

- Students cannot make consistent judgments about the instructor and instruction because of their immaturity, lack of experience, and capriciousness.
- Most student ranking schemes are nothing more than a popularity contest, with warm, friendly, humorous instructors emerging as winners every time.
- Students are not able to make accurate judgments until they have been away from the course for several years.
- Student ratings are both unreliable and invalid.
- The time and day the course is offered affects student ratings.
- Student ratings cannot be used meaningfully to improve instruction.

Studies and reviews of research on student ratings repeatedly disprove these myths:

> Student ratings are clearly multidimensional, quite reliable, reasonably valid, relatively uncontaminated by many variables often seen as sources of potential bias, and are seen to be useful by students, faculty and administrator....Probably students' evaluations of teaching effectiveness are the most thoroughly studied of all forms of personnel evaluation, and one of the best in terms of being supported by empirical research. (Marsh, 1987, p. 369)

Researchers have discovered some differences among student ratings of teachers in different academic fields and some slight associations between student ratings and class size, student rank, faculty rank, and whether the course is taken as an elective or requirement. Nevertheless, extensive research indicates that, although student ratings should be only one of several components in any faculty evaluation system, they offer a valuable perspective of teaching effectiveness. Systematic factor analysis of 75 years of student ratings reveals that most of the variation in student responses relate to four underlying dimensions—how *clear* and *interesting* the instructors' classes were perceived to be and how *positive* and *motivating* instructors were assessed to be in their interactions with students (Lowman, 1984, 1996).

In a study of junior faculty members in a well-known university, three of the participants observed that student comments in course evaluations were the deciding factors that led to their teaching improvement efforts. One faculty member observed: "I was kind of stubborn, at first. Then I realized later that things weren't working. So I had to change things. It's been a very slow, evolving process" (Stanley, 2002, p. 90).

Evaluations by Peers, Administrators, and External Judges

Research suggests that colleagues, administrators, and external judges can provide critical information about teaching effectiveness to supplement findings from student ratings. "Colleagues, particularly those from similar disciplines, can best judge content knowledge and other specialized aspects of teaching" (Centra, 1996, p. 51). Research also documents that students cannot accurately judge whether they are learning the "right" content and skills and that peers within the same discipline are needed to assess course material and teaching processes (Angelo, 1996). Furthermore, there are reports that colleagues also can be skillful observers of classroom teaching and can provide important feedback in the specific areas of instructor knowledge, method of instruction, instructor–student rapport, teaching behaviors, and enthusiasm (Seldin, 1988).

Holistic Evaluations

Newer approaches to assessing teaching effectiveness combine multiple perspectives and emphasize contextual and qualitative assessments of teaching—for example, the use of teaching portfolios. Portfolios typically include several sources of evaluative data and reflect the consensus that assessment requires multiple sources of data. Intended originally for peer review, portfolios provide opportunities for presenting examples of teaching, improving course planning and preparation, evaluating and giving feedback to students, and staying current in one's discipline area (Centra, 1996). One reason that teaching portfolios are growing in popularity is because they give faculty the opportunity to reflect on and voice their personal perspectives of how well they are succeeding in their teaching role: "Professors find the teaching portfolio process reaffirming because it involves them, perhaps for the first time, in self-reflection about their teaching" (Richlin & Manning, 1996, p. 65).

A campus-based research approach to qualitative evaluation of teaching is a group discussion technique known as *small group instructional diagnosis* (SGID). This evaluation technique uses small focus groups of students (six to eight students per group) to elicit feedback on three questions: "What do you like about the course?", "What would you like changed in the course?", and "What suggestions do you have for improving the course?" Researchers report dramatic effects on teaching improvement associated with SGID methods—in one study at a Washington state community college, 95 percent of the instructors made significant course-specific changes in response to student suggestions from these forums (Paulsen & Feldman, 1995).

Researchers indicate that these small group sessions allow faculty to evaluate classroom climate, rapport, and interaction, providing them information that they could not collect from any other source (Evertson & Green, 1986; Lewis, 1986, 1997). In a recent study of 10 university faculty members seriously involved in teaching development activities, 8 of the 10 agreed that the SGID technique and classroom observations helped them make the greatest improvements in their teaching. One of the participants in the university study observed, after using SGIDs half-way through the course: "The neat thing about mid-quarter evaluations is that you give students the feeling that you are trying to do something about the problems" (Stanley, 2002, p. 91).

The overwhelming message from researchers who emphasize the highly contextual process of teaching is to measure teaching by its products rather than its process. Growing ranks of college teaching researchers promote student learning as the appropriate yardstick for measuring teaching effectiveness. "Anything that helps students learn is good, effective teaching. Anything that hinders their learning is ineffective teaching" (Brookfield, 1990, p. 193).

Student Outcomes

The outcomes-based orientation toward measuring teaching effectiveness, unlike other assessment methods, is driven by forces outside the college. The focus on student outcomes has been the driving message in the national assessment movement in higher education in response to charges of inadequacies in and poor performance of undergraduate education, as was addressed earlier in the discussion of current institutional effectiveness issues. Perhaps as a result of at least a decade of increasing demands on colleges and universities to demonstrate accountability for the public dollars they receive (Ewell, 1994; Roueche et al., 1997; Ruppert, 1994), as many as 9 out of 10 U.S. colleges and universities have indicated that they are either implementing or planning a program of student-outcomes assessment (Banta, 1996).

As was discussed in earlier chapters, the shift to learning outcomes as the measure of teaching effectiveness is further reflected in a more recent emphasis on the concept that higher educational institutions should become "learning colleges" (O'Banion, 1996). Traditionally, colleges have viewed themselves as being in the business of *providing instruction,* and they measure teaching effectiveness on the basis of the quality of instruction provided by faculty. However, a growing perspective among some researchers and practitioners is that colleges exist to *produce learning* (Barr, 1995; Barr & Tagg, 1995; Boggs, 1996; Guskin, 1994; O'Banion, 1996). "To say that community colleges are in the business of providing instruction is equivalent to saying that auto companies are in the assembly line business. It is to say the method is the product" (Barr, 1995, p. 1). Assessing community colleges from the perspective of the *learning paradigm* raises questions about the community college's self-definition as the nation's premier teaching institution. These researchers emphasize that not all college learning takes place in the classroom, and they agree with the notion that "teaching without learning is just talking" (Angelo & Cross, 1993, p. 3).

Responses to "How Do You Know Learning Is Going On?"

Several of the 10 response categories for this question can be seen to fall into or overlap with a larger conceptual category, "observation and feedback." It is important to realize this while reading the responses across different categories. For example, a teacher who is listening to students engaged in group work is also engaged in observation and verbal feedback; a teacher who receives a third-person report from an employer is also engaged in written feedback; and so on.

Formal Testing

Formal tests occupied the top position in the list of most frequently used testing tools. However, careful analysis of survey and focus group comments revealed that the traditional formats we associate with formal testing procedures—for example, true/false, multiple-choice, and fill-in-the-blank questions—were being looked at with new eyes by the majority of these faculty. Faculty observed that even traditional tests such as multiple-choice or even short-answer tests (by paper and pencil or by word processing) could be designed better to reveal what and how well students have learned. Moreover, they observed that the *timing* of any test could be critical to how effectively and accurately it measured learning.

Techniques for (1) "taking learning's pulse" and (2) "changing direction or speed" of instruction were frequent, more informal variations on more traditional testing procedures. Pre- and post-tests, occurring early and late in the semester, before and after single content or skill units or as regular, timely, formative, and summative checks on learning, were popular strategies. Included in the pre- and post-test categories were some familiar classroom assessment techniques (Cross & Angelo, 1988), including the "Minute Paper." Also, some variations on the "Punctuated Lecture" (Cross & Angelo, 1988) technique appeared as strategies for "touching base" and "taking pulse" during class (as is illustrated, for example, in the last response in the list).

Multiple choice tests *can* require critical thinking.

When essay tests occur in the semester is important; essays are much better indicators of how well students are learning when they come toward the end of the semester and students can show their knowledge of the course content and their ability to spell and use good grammar.

Before dismissing any class, I require students to write one or two sentences explaining something they learned in class that day.

Students must submit a question about something they did not understand or about which they want/need more information before they leave the classroom.

Sometime during the class, I ask students to stop taking notes or working in their groups and explain, in writing, exactly what they were learning, how they were learning it, and how certain they were the learning strategy was working.

Applications

Clearly, the respondents' focus on evaluating students' abilities to apply what they have learned indicated that application is regarded as a critical assessment tool. One respondent wrote that his college defines assessment as "obtaining and documenting demonstrable and measurable evidence of learning outcomes." He tells his students: "If I can't see you do it, I can't give you credit for it." History has been his teaching discipline for more than 30 years! Moreover, we were fascinated by the number of observations that learning applications occur on the teacher's side of the desk, as the last two responses in the list illustrate.

> Students who have to write responses to "what if" questions must think beyond the standard answers—they have to use the information they have, or the skill they have developed in a new setting, or in a setting characteristic of others we have used in class.

> I know that learning is happening when students begin to make connections to their own experiences.

> I teach computer applications; either they can do it, or they can't. If they can't, I have to help them until they understand (easy for me).

> Asking essay questions that require application of content are high on my list for finding out whether students can really perform.

> I am just beginning to develop rubrics; I have always known what they were, but now I am finding out how important they can be to my students when, for example, they make oral presentations to the class.

> I was content with having only the basic computer skills until I realized how important going beyond the basics was for my students; now, I'm only one step in front of them to "lead the way," and they're gaining on me. But, I'm getting better all the time—and, lucky for me and for them, so are they.

Verbal and Written Feedback

Respondents indicated that they actively seek feedback from students and from other faculty in the college or employers in the community who have had opportunities to evaluate students in follow-on courses or jobs.

> At the end of the term, I ask my students to tell me, anonymously, about the most effective teaching technique I have used during the course. And, of course, I must ask to hear about the least effective technique, too.

> I talk to students outside of class—and not only in my office during office hours! I

believe many of us have become friends. They are really honest with you under those circumstances.

I stay in good touch with colleagues who have my students in their classes after they have had a class with me; what they tell me keeps me on my toes and honest!

Nonverbal Feedback

Faculty reported a multitude of ways in which they developed multiple observation strategies for staying tuned to student behaviors that can signal that learning is or is not occurring. The following statements embrace the common elements among their perspectives.

I feel that I can "tune in" to students by watching their expressions; I validate my observations when I evaluate their written work.

I can tell that my students are feeling more comfortable as the semester progresses; they learn better in a more relaxed setting.

I can tell by the look in their eyes—the engaged expressions are undeniable testimony to their involvement and interest.

When students change the ways in which they revise and edit their papers, the progress they are making is obvious.

I stand in different places in the room; I do not always stand at the front; I can really make my most useful observations this way.

Sparks fly as the discussion of legal cases becomes more intense. The group flows as heads shake, bodies lean forward, questions are asked, resources are quoted and shared.

Their eyes will tell you—you're going too fast, or they didn't get the idea. If the eyes are shut, your job is to find out why. If their eyes are clear and alive, they are involved.

The "ah ha's" have it; they follow successfully completed assignments; they precede positive responses to the next questions.

Students simply cannot fake real excitement!

Students want to come to class—EXCELLENT!

Helping and Teaching Others, Group Work

Relationships between and among students are interesting developments to watch and underscore the power of the notion: "pay to be a tutor, not to be tutored" (McKeachie, 1994, p. 146).

When a student can explain a concept to another student accurately, especially when it involves the extension of a concept to a new application, both students are getting a good lesson.

My students start to teach each other while waiting for me to get around to their groups. I hear my own phrases and examples being correctly reapplied in "THEIR teaching."

Sometimes I ask students to teach *me* a theory, a concept, an idea, or a solution to a problem.

Students ask questions beyond the scope of the instruction or the assignment; they have thought more broadly than that.

Students turn in assignments that are better and demanded more work of them than I required.

Students demonstrate less satisfaction with their first or second drafts; they continue to work toward higher goals than I had set for them.

Students form their own study groups and engage in meetings outside of class.

What students tell me—and don't tell me—in their self-evaluations can tell me a lot about what they really learned.

I know learning is going on when students challenge each others' opinions.

Outside-of-Class Interactions and Third-Person Reports

However, respondents admitted that they especially savored the serendipitous feedback that comes unexpectedly and confirms their beliefs that all of their efforts have made a difference in students' lives:

Students come back and tell me about lectures or assignments that they still remember semesters or years later.

Students share the most intimate details of their experiences—often, they tell me that they thought they could never love this subject or that they were not smart enough to ever "get it."

Employers call me to encourage my students to apply at their law firms because they have former students of mine as employees.

Students tell their peers to take my class.

Many students contact me after graduation and keep me up to date on their careers and their families.

Students leave the class discussing, arguing, laughing—all behaviors and emotions related to what happened in class that day.

My colleagues, faculty and counselors both, tell me that they hear my class is first-rate—I consider that a good clue that I'm doing just fine!

We Don't [Know]

Finally, some respondents indicated that assessment remains a mystery and an enormous problem—that they don't know whether learning is going on or not.

We don't know [if students are learning]. A former student told me that we were not good judges of what/whether students had learned.

It is especially difficult in the humanities and history.

If you have to ask, then you don't know and won't!

Sometimes, I don't.

Often, I don't know if they are learning what I want them to learn, but I know they are getting something.

I want them to get the big picture and my developmental math students have a very difficult time synthesizing and summarizing their knowledge.

Conclusion

A little girl was asked by her teacher to name the king whose daughter's marriage made possible the unification of Denmark and Norway in 1380. The student said,

> "Wow, that's the kind of question that makes your temples throb. It makes your ears ring and your hair stand on end. It makes your eyes water and your cheeks burn, your mouth turn dry and teeth ache. A question like that can destroy your whole head."…the problem for us is making sure that we ask ourselves the right questions. (Owens, 1991, p. 58)

Choosing the right questions to ask is critical; it is step one in choosing the criteria by which to assess learning and to know, for sure, whether or not learning has occurred. No one ever said that the questions would not make "…temples throb…ears ring and …hair stand on end." But colleges cannot let these questions "destroy [their] whole head."

Our assessment question for these respondents was not designed, nor did we intend, to probe the enormous depths of the assessment issues. For example, we did not ask about test construction, or criteria by which to evaluate essay answers, or the particulars of verbal feedback techniques. Clearly, the possible responses to more probing questions could have taken us far beyond the scope of this study, but no doubt could have been enlightening and fascinating. However, we did get the flavor of assessment issues alive in this cohort group, and with that flavor we learned or reminded ourselves of at least four things.

One, the majority of assessment research—that is, how well we can assess what students are learning and how well we identify what they should be learning—tells us, simply, that we are not there yet! Generally, the conceptual frameworks of tying mission statements to outcomes that are being advanced in the literature on institutional effectiveness simply are not being adopted on any large scale. A recent study of institutional effectiveness measures and outcomes in community colleges documented that, on the whole, these institutions still do not collect the appropriate data to tell them whether or not they are achieving their goals (Roueche et al., 1997).

Similar to reports from numerous studies of teaching development in institutions of higher education, many of our respondents described a diversity of assessment strategies and techniques; however, our findings generally reflect this conclusion: There is a dearth of meaningful assessment. By and large, colleges are unable to say with any certainty whether students have learned what the professors are teaching. This is particularly true of abilities such as critical thinking that develop across the confines of individual courses. The absence of explicit descriptions of the outcomes desired hampers assessment. So, too, do the independent treatment of individual courses and faculty unfamiliarity with meaningful assessment methods. Without knowing how well students have learned, the faculty finds it difficult to improve education in any purposeful way. This lack of assessment data can frustrate the desire to lift performance expectations (AACU, 2002, p.18).

All in all, our analysis of responses provided good evidence that the light is getting brighter as we move through the assessment tunnel, although arguably we have a long way to go. The faculty who participated in this study described experiments, adaptations, and adoptions of an array of assessment strategies. Had we asked, specifically, about what is being taught or what skills were being developed or what competency levels students should achieve; the criteria by which the content, skills, or competency levels have been identified as appropriate; and the criteria against which learning outcomes were evaluated, we would have been into a much larger, if not enormous, study. However, what we did learn from a number of responses that went beyond what we were asking in our query—How do you know learning is going on?—is that discussions and policy development conversations are being held with some regularity and across this country around these issues. Clearly, faculty are using some of the strategies they support to improve student learning—especially obvious in their descriptions of collaborative faculty activities within and between disciplines, between programs and stakeholders.

Two, we know that problems, primarily those created by assessment language, definitions, and procedures, with which colleges are grappling are further complicated by the lack of both credible, useful, improved models and more resources to support experimentation (Wilson, Miles, Baker, & Schoenberger, 2000). Colleges interested in learning outcomes need help documenting student achievement at all levels, in all classes, across the institution. Colleges committed to verifying learning outcomes may best choose to focus on smaller units initially, funneling all of their interest on single steps or in specific departments or programs.

Three, we know that LEARNING IS OCCURRING ALL THE TIME. It does not have an on-off button. In families, either children learn that they are neither loved nor valued, or they may learn that they may have a support group for life. In colleges, students may learn that they cannot learn, that teachers do not have any significant interest in their work or their progress, that the college classroom is not a comfortable place to be, or that what they are being taught is not relevant or useful to any other part of their lives. Or, they learn that they are capable of learning, that there are teachers who have a genuine interest in their success and who "pull out all of the stops" to help them achieve it.

Finally, what we know for sure is that the outcomes of learning—both the intended and the possibly unintended—should be factors in any discussion of the critical question: Of what significance is this decision, action, policy, and the like to student success? College administrators and faculty simply must make every effort to ensure that students' experiences on their watch are as positive as opportunity, support, and effort can effect; that content is appropriate; that demonstrated skills meet expectations; and that teaching and learning, assessed regularly, meet the highest standards possible for quality and performance.

Chapter Eight

Information Technology in Instruction

It gets late early out there.

—Yogi Berra

This New York Yankee great described a curious situation, common at Yankee Stadium, when long and heavy shadows would descend over the players and the grounds every evening just before dusk, creating the illusion that the appearance of moon and stars was but a moment away. We were intrigued by how appropriate his description was to describing community colleges' race to get their collective arms around the information technology (IT) explosion, embracing questions about what and how much technology they can afford and use effectively to support and improve instruction and services, as the various technologies simultaneously expand features and capabilities at rapid-fire pace. Caught up in a race for the appropriate balance of opportunities and outcomes, colleges watch as developing technologies increase challenges and odds for institutions struggling to be competitive, to increase market share, and to achieve a conscionable bottom line of justifiable expenditures of human and fiscal resources to make good on their mission and achieve their goals.

Because the participants in this study received their awards for demonstrated teaching ability, as a group they were more likely to exhibit a rich mix of opinions about and experiences with IT than had they been chosen from a group of "true believers." Their diverse perspectives could give us a more balanced and realistic view of how, why, when, and with whom IT could be applied than had they all been strong individual advocates of incorporating or expanding technology in the classroom. It was a robust harvest of high-quality perspectives that we sought to gather and share. Furthermore, in light of the current flurry of discussions about IT, faculty perspectives about the *value* that current IT applications add to instruction are critical data to which colleges should attend in making future investment decisions. We asked award recipients two questions regarding the current use of IT in instruction (questions #5 and #6—see Appendix B):

- In what ways do you use information technology in instruction?
- What do you see as the key issues (positives or problems) in the use of technology in instruction?

At this juncture, it is important for us to note that our analysis to the responses to these questions draws from a monograph published by the League for Innovation in the Community College. In *Technology, Learning, and Community (TLC)*, Milliron and Miles (1998) provided us with a useful template for the chapters in this book, generally, and a considerable amount of thought and effort that could be improved on only by a few recent reports of discovery and implementation by other excellent faculty, specifically. We appreciated having such an excellent monograph on which to expand as we wrote this book.

We found that faculty perceptions regarding IT and instruction could be grouped into the same three conceptual clusters that Milliron and Miles used in their monograph. In the next section, we present an overview and analysis of responses to question #5, which focus on technology use. We then present an overview and analysis of responses to the second technology question, "What do you see as the key issues (positives or problems) in the use of technology in instruction?" in two separate sections, because the 12 response categories for this question (see Appendix B) could be further categorized as being either learning-related or community-related key issues in the use of technology.

Responses to "In What Ways Do You Use Information Technology in Instruction?"

We need not look far to see the changes that the IT explosion has brought to all educational institutions, at all levels. In particular, we point to the expanded and continuing interest in the use of technology to improve teaching and learning as seen in the increasing numbers of related topics appearing in conference programs internationally. The League for Innovation's annual Conference on Information Technology (CIT) has grown from 550 participants in its first year (1984) to more than 4,000 participants in 2002.

In the early days, the technology conference sessions dealt primarily with issues of administrative computing and technical infrastructures. Instructional issues were primarily focused on whether students should be encouraged to "compose on the keyboard" in writing classes, for example, or rather be required to continue putting pen to paper, further strengthening the mental processes required to put thoughts together and make them visible. Currently, the program submissions related to technology applications for teaching and learning outnumber all other topics by a ratio of 9 to 1.

As well, the number of sessions focused on technology and application doubled between 1998 and 2002 at NISOD's annual Conference on Teaching and Leadership Excellence. Clearly, the use of technology to improve and expand instructional options is gathering interest from those who are beginning to think more about how to infuse technology into instruction to improve teaching and learning and how to support that infusion. Questions about the costs associated with developing technology infrastructures and innovative financial support initiatives and strategies are generating critical follow-on discussions. All are hot topics in the large majority of documents publicizing conferences, no matter their size or their target audience.

And even as the depth and breadth of issues and questions have changed radically over the last few years, the technology that conference participants use to present and embellish their information has changed, as well. There are fewer video data projectors and more interactive technologies—for example, computer-aided instruction and the World Wide Web. Presenters describe students' improved access to information, to multiple uses of interactive tutorial materials, threaded discussions, bulletin-board services, chat rooms, net meetings, and other options that free up everyone from more place- and time-bound models of education.

However, this enormous increase in interest and practice is countered, understandably, by voices warning against moving too quickly or without adequate, reasoned, informed forethought and planning. They urge disciplined steps toward change and yet simultaneously warn that these steps must be accelerated to avoid being left behind. Yogi Berra described well the arena where colleges currently find themselves; they are being required to learn on the job, while teaching what they are learning and using what they are learning to teach. At the same time, understandably and as expected, the monetary and human costs associated with these efforts are major issues.

The IT conundrum has brought out strong voices of support, caution, and opposition (e.g., Pedersen, 2002; Pittinsky, 2002). The conflicting arguments from strong advocates within the institution that support embracing technology's applications across campuses and those arguments from more cautious and critical opponents are all poignant and justified. The voices of caution warn that change in any arena is difficult, and we should not fail to recognize that "countless proponents of 'inevitable' change" should not underestimate or fail "to appreciate the powerful cultural forces that work against any radical transformation in teaching methods or the collegiate experience" (Pedersen, 2002, p. 15). Taken together, they demonstrate the need for holding up critical, contentious issues to a bright light to discern the particulars of their parts for reasoned discussion and careful weighing.

Student Application and Production

One of the more intriguing findings of our study is that the most common uses of technology in instruction cited by respondents is not instructor-based but rather student-based. They identified technology for student application and production as their number one choice for using technology in instruction. Several faculty members noted that students can use technology tools to engage in research, meaningful inquiry, as well as to produce professional-quality print publications, multimedia presentations, interactive CD-ROMs, and custom Web sites. Moreover, in creating products and conducting research, students can share what they are learning with their classmates.

> I get students on computers to file sample incident reports in Criminal Justice class and produce formal documents.

> Groups work together to produce PowerPoint presentations and Web sites on course topics.

> Students use computer-based writing software to collaborate on composition and editing.

> I assign research projects that require students to give/gather information using technology.

> I expect all work to look professional; I have students use word processors, spreadsheets, and PowerPoint to prepare their assignments to make sure it does.

> I require technology use in their oral presentations. I often require group oral reports using PowerPoint, and they replace some of the more conventional papers that I usually require.

Student-Driven Learning

The second most common technology application reported by faculty was technology for student-driven learning—whether constructed by faculty using authoring programs or prepared by software or publishing houses, students could use technological tools to engage in such learning activities as computer-based tutorials, Web sites, and multimedia programs.

Students are encouraged to use "tutoring" computer programs available in our math center.

Students use software that accompanies the text for supplementary drills.

I construct puzzles on class content using a puzzle maker program.

Students are encouraged to take a computerized "student behavior inventory," which asks questions about study skills, time management, test taking, etc., and gives students a printout of results and ways to improve.

There are some self-paced computer programs on some of our syllabi content. Students can do these programs in the computer lab and come to class prepared to move beyond the program in a higher-level discussion on that topic.

I encourage individual computer practice for licensing exams to increase comfort levels with exam construction, time limits, and computer use.

Presentation

The third most common cluster of technology applications for instruction was technology for presentation. Focus group faculty mentioned technology applications, such as PowerPoint, World Wide Web, CD-ROMs, and multimedia carts, that they use regularly as standard teaching tools; they observed that such tools help bring curriculum to life with stimulating visuals and intriguing strategies for putting information into use contexts.

PowerPoint is a God-send.

I use PowerPoint and ToolBook presentations for all formal lectures and give students copies of outlines prior to class.

We put lectures and overheads on WWW.

I use the Internet to present interactive material in class to spark discussion.

I have found that graphing calculators in higher levels of math classes can really give students a concrete picture of what's happening. The calculators do not replace analytical skills; rather, they reinforce them through a "visual confirmation" of their analysis.

I use interactive CD-ROM programs in the classroom and have them available for students to use/review in the computer learning lab.

I teach in a "smart classroom"—state of the art. I often use the Internet for much of my teaching.

I take advantage of the interactive math Web sites and use them regularly in my teaching.

I put all of my teaching materials and handouts on the Web, even students' attendance and grade sheets.

I utilize a Web site that accompanies the text and require students to turn in at least two online activities from it each semester.

Communication and Interactions

The subsequent cluster of technology applications includes technology tools to improve communication between students and faculty, and between and among students—using e-mail, bulletin boards, Listservs®, electronic forums, and real-time chats. Such interactive tools give instructors diverse options for reaching transitory, busy students. Moreover, faculty reported using these tools to contact, collaborate, and share information with other educators in and out of their discipline areas. They observe that these expanded opportunities to reach other educators help them avoid or at least significantly reduce the challenges of discipline isolation.

I use e-mail to send and receive comments and papers from students.

We encourage students to use e-mail to communicate with each other and with the instructor. We hope that using e-mail in this way will foster a sense of personal responsibility for learning.

Distance learning is a marvelous tool for doing role-plays, sharing information that is real-world oriented.

I use "groupware" to hold and facilitate electronic meetings.

I use e-mail and subscriptions to listservs to communicate with other teachers around the world with similar teaching issues to discuss and problems to solve.

Research and Reference

Focus group faculty also identified a number of applications of technology for research and reference. They explained that they frequently direct students to a variety of new research and reference technologies. They described how library databases, virtual textbooks, and the World Wide Web leave the Dewey decimal system behind and enable students to search for and manipulate information in ways only dreamed of by their predecessors. And, they reported how they use these research tools to keep up with current trends in their discipline area.

I teach a web-based developmental writing class. I have worked with the librarian to develop library assignments, which focus on teaching students how to judge Internet sites and articles on periodical databases for research.

I suggest that students use the Internet to do research for both oral and written reports.

Internet sites can inform pre-law students of school programs, admissions standards, law school admission test preparation courses, and access to particular information from law school libraries on agency decisions and case law.

Information via technology is a critical learning tool. The Internet is great to use for research purposes, especially for those who teach at branch campuses that have limited library and other research materials.

My students and I use Internet sites to access specific, up-to-date information on state/local government agencies, progress of legislation, and access legislators' e-mail addresses.

Internet research is valuable for students and for me.

Course Management and Assessment

Course management and assessment technologies are changing the ways that faculty organize their instructional materials and evaluate student progress. Some faculty are creating dynamic syllabi that are available on internal college networks or over the Internet. Faculty use computer-adaptive testing, virtual teaching assistants, spreadsheets, databases, and online course staging technologies to manage information in new ways for themselves and for students. Some faculty suggested that grade books are giving way to on-demand performance indicators available on a Web site 24 hours a day. Given the complexities of teaching and the challenges of becoming more learning-centered, faculty suggest that these tools could not have come at a better time:

All class notes are available on our class Web site.

Distance learning students videotape their speeches for evaluation.

Students use e-mail to send in papers and receive comments.

I hold virtual office hours, using e-mail and chat rooms.

I have a Web site for my syllabus, I use PowerPoint to organize my lecture material, and I use e-mail to give and receive assignments.

I use QuestionMark software to design and deliver testing online.
Through computer-based testing, I can provide real-time feedback to my distance learning students.

Conclusions About the Use of Information Technology in Instruction

The range of technology tools available to educators and the options and opportunities they provide for instruction is impressive. However, judging from the responses to our questions, even these award recipients are only beginning to embrace and implement new technology. For example, the clusters of technology for course management and technology for assessment were identified as key categories of instructional technology application by focus group faculty, but few survey respondents reported using these tools (only 31 percent and 14 percent, respectively). Moreover, several of the instructional presentation technologies mentioned by faculty involve more dated tools such as overhead projectors, VCRs, and 35-millimeter slide projectors. A number of faculty admitted that they felt somewhat behind the times, and one survey respondent added this apology: "I don't use technology to any great extent in my classes, except for some word processing and spell-check. I'm sorry. There is just so much to learn."

Nonetheless, teaching excellence award recipients are integrating technology into their instruction in growing numbers. One participant explained that faculty were slow to adopt new technology because they see it as unreliable. Many in that particular focus group expressed their agreement, best captured in this comment: "Only recently have many of these tools become stable enough for a teacher to trust that it wouldn't break down in the middle of class. Now I'm ready to use this stuff!" Most interesting, however, was the finding that the two most prevalent uses of technology for instruction involved the student as the primary user—for application and production, and for student-driven learning. This observation suggests that successful community college faculty are demonstrating the finding from years of research on good teaching—excellent faculty are those who actively engage the student in the learning process (Cross, 1998).

Responses Focusing on Learning as a Key Issue in Using Technology

Having said all of that, it is clear that the technology revolution and the learning revolution are on parallel paths: IT is alive and well to various degrees and at different levels, on college campuses everywhere. Discussions abound that learning must be improved and expanded in diverse, innovative, and meaningful ways, that student diversity and increasing hunger for relevant learning experiences create powerful opportunities for colleges focused on becoming more learning-centered. Colleges could determine their progress toward that end by measuring against these key characteristics of learning colleges:

> …(1) programs and services create substantive change in individual learners; (2) learners are engaged as full partners in the learning process, assuming primary responsibility for their own choices; (3) there are as many options for learning as possible; (4) learners are assisted in forming and participating in collaborative learning activities; (5) the role of learning facilitator is defined by the needs of the learner; (6) all college employees identify with their role in supporting learning; and (7) success is measured by documented, improved, and expanded learning for learners. (O'Banion, 1997, p. 2)

The intensifying focus on learning as the primary teaching goal—hence, the over-arching goal of community colleges—has great potential for transforming higher education. Combined with the focus on learning, the focus on the potential power, utility, and flexibility of IT can help colleges respond better to changing educational needs of our information-based society. That focus, however, is tempered by several sensitive learning challenges; one such challenge is what has been referred to as the "support service crisis" (Gilbert, 1997). As colleges respond to students' demands for more sophisticated learning options, as faculty strive to apply new instructional tools, and as employers seek graduates skilled in IT, community colleges are pressed to keep faculty and staff up to speed. Clearly, IT promises increased learning options for students, and students will need these emerging, vital skills in continuing their studies and in their workplaces. Information technology is becoming a new basic skills requirement in many community colleges (de los Santos, de los Santos, & Milliron, 2001; Milliron & Miles, 2001).

A set of learning-related issues—learning for students and faculty—emerged from responses to the question about key issues in the use of technology in instruction.

Technology Is a Basic Skill That Students Need

The highest-ranking response reiterates an observation that learning about technology itself is becoming essential; it is a "basic skill" our students need. Debates about technology no longer focus primarily on costs and productivity but rather on the reality that IT skills have become a core learning component for community college students, whether they plan to go on to a four-year institution or go directly into the workplace. More than 98 percent of our national sample of award recipients agreed with this major premise.

> The future is upon us. Every house will be connected by fiber optics in the next five to ten years. Students, for employment in the future, will need to be technologically competent.

> With technology becoming an integral part of the industry, the students need to be introduced to these concepts before entering the workforce.

> Students will be exposed to high tech on their first job. They must use current technology to succeed.

> Technology prepares students for the present and what will be dominant for the rest of their lives.

> We must ensure that students have basic skills in technology and are comfortable before expecting more.

> Students, by using computers (word processing, Internet access, etc.) for my classes, learn or strengthen skills they will, in all likelihood, need in their work.

Use of Technology Requires Time and Training

The next key learning-related issue focused on the faculty's own learning; participants contended that technology had become so complex and changed so quickly that they found it difficult to remain current or keep "up to speed." Most respondents agreed that it takes a lot of time and training to use it well.

Technology changes so fast that staying current is difficult.

We lack the time to train to use technology. We have [training] classes, but at times it's difficult for me to attend.

I learn new software every semester; at times my head is spinning!

Problem: When in hell do we have the time to produce the damn slide slow?

Faculty loads make it difficult to give technology the time necessary to create or use this resource to our best advantage.

Unless you really understand the mechanics, you and your students can get really frustrated.

Technology Can Make Teaching More Engaging

Even with training issues, most faculty agreed that technology helps make teaching and learning more engaging. Respondents concur with the observation that "community college students are becoming more accustomed to information technology, and they expect the associated innovations to be a part of their educational experiences" (Johnson, 1997, p. 2). Focus group faculty noted that multimedia presentation technologies, interactive communication tools, student-driven learning options, and a host of other technological capabilities help students connect to learning in new ways.

It can capture students' interests and make otherwise dull information come alive for them.

Using technology adds dimension to subject matter. Away with using only the written page for instruction!

I can show invasive or private activities that students may avoid (peri care) or not have an opportunity to experience (surgery).

It gives me the ability to make the classroom or the course work experience more exciting.

It gives students the ability to "see" the material to be learned.

I can show how the normal curve superimposes the histogram for some distribution. Demonstrate the probability of an event by showing the integration of the curve. Show the regression line that passes through the scatter plot.

Technology opens up opportunities to bring real-time examples into the classroom—e.g., in nursing, technology allows the student to "see and hear" the patient.

It helps add clarity—makes visual what is abstract on the page.

Technology Facilitates Different Kinds of Learning

Moreover, faculty noted that when used well, technology can help facilitate different kinds of learning. They pointed out that the connection capabilities that IT makes possible enhance interactive and collaborative learning. Sophisticated presentation technologies and skillful management of information by instructors could stimulate different learning styles and illuminate intricate or perplexing concepts. Respondents noted that students' use of technology tools to access and analyze information helped them develop critical thinking skills and foster the construction of knowledge. More than 92 percent of the surveyed faculty agreed that differentiated learning was enhanced by technology.

"When used well" is an important phrase to remember. With it, respondents reminded us that IT use in education—even when highlighted by elaborate Web sites, chat rooms, and interactive video—does not equate with or automatically create good teaching. The challenges are to keep a strong focus on learning processes and outcomes and to document improved and expanded learning.

Technology gives students more avenues of learning—some are readers and some are watchers and some are listeners.

It is another way to teach students with different learning styles.

It reinforces and stimulates all "senses" for learning.

It provides different methods of instruction to students with varied learning styles.

Technology allows students another avenue to learn.

It allows learners to show their skills and become a peer teacher in a community of teachers/learners.

It enhances learning by appealing to different types of learners.

A picture is worth a thousand words—multiple methods of learning.

Technology Gives Students More Control Over Learning

Faculty addressed the issue that effective technology use appeals to all students, no matter their learning styles, and it gives students more control of their learning, particularly through asynchronous options such as computer-based tutorials and Web-supported materials. Such technologies, faculty say, are giving new meaning to the more traditional concepts of self-paced learning.

Technology offers cutting-edge ways to allow students to follow and expand their own ideas.

Video material can be stopped, started, segmented, or whole to make a point.

Students take responsibility for their own learning.

Students can take a greater part in their learning.

The information age is realized in instruction—rather than being told this is the information age, students actively participate in developing the age.

Students can learn at their own pace when they can access technology in and out of the traditional classroom.

It allows for individual adjustment—e.g., slower students can spend time as needed in hands-on learning.

It allows the faster ones to move on, keep interested, get more value for the education.

Some Are Tempted to Use Technology for the Novelty

One major learning challenge associated with the learning options offered by IT that was emphasized repeatedly by faculty is that some instructors are tempted to use technology for its novelty, rather than utility. Respondents stressed that without a sharp focus on the intended purpose of enhancing learning, technology use can easily deteriorate into what one faculty member called "the gee whiz factor," with little or no learning to show for the many hours of effort.

Too much "entertainment" and "fun" may actually slow down or minimize serious learning or just "miss the point."

There may be more focus on gadgets than on students and learning.

Overuse of technology becomes a crutch to teaching rather than a supplement to or addition to taught information.

Too many instructors try to use technology for the sake of using technology. If it will not enhance the learning, don't use it.

Support is more concerned with technological efficiency than effectiveness for teaching. It's simply technology for the sake of technology.

Students can be dazzled by the method and ignore the content.

Responses Focusing on Community as a Key Issue in Using Technology

Maintaining a sense of community was high on our participants' list of critical "keepers"—the attitudes and opportunities that could make IT work in instruction. Much has been said about the negative aspects of technology, particularly its capacity to separate and to disconnect. Milliron and Miles (1998), authors of *TLC,* retold a story that Ed Hollowell, a professor and psychiatrist at the Harvard Medical School, shared in his address to the 1997 Teaching, Learning, and Technology Roundtable Institute. Hollowell's remarks underscored the critical nature of maintaining the human touch in the information age. He explained that although we have more opportunities than ever to make contacts with other individuals and entities, we also have more feelings of disconnectedness, and we feel the loss of meaningful contact with friends, family, and social organizations. The effect of technology on the mind, body, spirit, and community has been a frequent subject of conversations among theologians, philosophers, educators, and researchers (e.g., Healy, 1994; Mander, 1992).

Hollowell related a story about a professor demonstrating the concept of being "full" to a physics class. The professor places a number of large rocks into a cylindrical container until it can hold no more and then asks the class if the container is full. The cylinder looks full, so the class casually responds in the affirmative. But, the professor takes a bucket of gravel and pours it into the container until the smaller stones settle into the spaces among the larger rocks. He then stares at the class as they looked a bit stunned at missing the obvious, and asks again, "Now, is it full?" The class again replies, "Yes." Then the professor takes out a bucket of sand and pours sand into the seemingly full container, and the sand weaves through all the crevices and up to the top of the cylinder. He then winks at the class and repeats his question. The class sighs somewhat hesitatingly, "Yes, now it's full." But, once again, the professor reaches down, this time producing a bucket of water, which he slowly pours into the container until it gurgles to the cylinder's lip. He places the four empty buckets next to the cylinder and smiles at the class, "You see, we can fit all this into one space. But, it is not as easy as it might seem. The trick is to remember to put the big things in first" (Milliron & Miles, 1998, p. 27).

Of course, Hollowell's point is central to the idea of community—that we can do whatever we wish about and around technology as long as we remember to "put the big things in first." In our efforts to build learning communities, we talk about fostering and supporting human contact and relationships, about focusing on the "big things" that the technology should be helping us achieve. We should not allow the minutiae of e-mail, voicemail, and Web sites, for example, to overwhelm the space that should be taken up with the "big rocks" of relationships, connectors, and learning.

Students should be involved with others and with the institution, should have a sense of connectedness that is critical to any student's decision to stay (Tinto, 1987). We know the value of involvement and its relationship to learning; we hear it in students' stories and in their praise for the people who make institutions human, who make a difference in students' lives. We would be surprised to hear students bestow similar praise on a software program, a Web site, or a PC. It is the human connections, the human side of the learning process, in which we must embrace and engage technology.

Hollowell's advice that we should be about "putting the big things in first" was echoed in the discussions regarding building communities of learners and fostering the human contacts and relationships that support learning. We need to focus on the "big things" that technology should be helping us achieve, and we need to be careful with the minutia of e-mail, voicemail, threaded discussions, and the like, and not allow them to overtake the space intended for relationships and connections among and between students, faculty, and the college.

Technology Can Get Very Expensive

Among the issues that faculty identified is that technology for instruction can get very expensive. Serious budgetary implications for technology can test the most cooperative and friendly of college communities. Faculty told tales of technology "money pits" and disputes over allocations and resources. Institutional relationships frequently suffer; faculty made these observations about how technology issues can affect the college community.

Training needs to be a budgeted item just like equipment and software.

There are not enough computers! My office mate and I share one, and we both use PowerPoint!

There is serious frustration in not having the resources to create what I know can be done.

Our classrooms are built for the 60s, not the 90s or the 21st century.

Computer labs are expensive to set up and become outdated the day of the grand opening; they're also expensive to maintain.

There is unequal access to technology—some faculty have the latest computer and printer in their private office; others are in a broom closet with three other faculty and antiquated technology where they have to beg and borrow computer time here and there, stopping and starting their work and going from one word processor such as WordPerfect to another such as Word on a different computer.

Students Don't Have Equal Access to Technology

In addition, faculty reminded us to avoid leaving others behind in our zeal to move forward with technology. Participants pointed out that community colleges can be the gateways to IT for everyone, but we must face the challenge that students do not have equal access to technology. They noted that we must create technology infrastructures that can be shared and from which students can benefit equitably.

Not all students have access to computers/Internet either on or off campus.

Using e-mail with students allows them to communicate with me outside their classroom, both locally and globally, but they have to have e-mail to participate.

WE CAN'T LEAVE ANYONE OUT—what about those students who don't have computers?

The Internet is great, if you can get to it.

We need technology accessibility for everyone.

Hardware and Software Can Be Problematic

We heard multiple discussions about the ubiquitous hardware and software problems that frustrate educators trying to adapt to the new technologies. They echo Gonick and Milliron's (2002) argument that the stress created by technical instabilities and failures can be enormous; the challenges of technology unreliability must be addressed in order to improve the chances that faculty can be convinced of the value of using technology in the classroom.

Hardware/software problems are very time-consuming and distracting.

Classroom use of technology demands a back-up plan, as it is prone to crashing.

You must plan ahead and be prepared for the unexpected— you *will* have technology problems.

A lot of the "bugs" have not been worked out—valuable class time can be lost because equipment, computers, etc., do not function properly.

Damned stuff does not always work.

Problems Caused by Fear, Resistance, and True Believers

The problems associated with the technology further fuel the fire of fear and resistance about the use of technology. Resistance to any change or new initiative is to be expected; it is also important to expect that the major cause of the resistance is fear. Study participants observed that technology conjures up a number of fears for faculty: experiencing technophobia, appearing ignorant in front of peers and students, failing after relinquishing proven traditional teaching approaches, or losing control of the classroom. Students experience many of these fears, as well.

Moreover, battle lines are drawn across the college when advocates and resisters begin to argue the merits of applying technology to instruction, in particular. Respondents noted that "true believers" can cause problems by "promising the moon in a minute," when most faculty are struggling just to get the technology to their class on time. The stress is particularly acute when the technologically savvy behave in a condescending or contemptuous manner toward the technical neophytes. The challenges these situations pose for colleges were reflected in faculty's comments.

Instructors refuse to change with the times.

Students excited about technology may have frustrations because instructors are behind the times.

There is resistance to learning new techniques—both students and faculty, but more faculty.

Some teachers are still scared.

Too many colleagues fear technology.

Technology frightens students with little or no exposure.

Technology can be intimidating to the nontraditional student. This intimidation could hurt learning. It has been my experience that older women are terribly afraid of computers.

One problem is techno-able folks patronizing the techno-novice. No one wants to learn something they have been made to feel inadequate about.

The Need to Keep the Human Touch

The final and most substantive community-related technology issue revolves around maintaining the human touch while using technology in instruction. Focus group faculty observed that the complex world of the community college—with its student diversity and its multiple missions—makes it unique in its struggles with technology and its effectiveness in instruction. This context requires that community colleges craft technology-based policies and designs carefully. Faculty constantly returned to the question: "What are the telltale communication signs of confusion or effectiveness in an online course?" They repeatedly turned to the issues of how important nonverbal communication had become in their classrooms as gauges of student learning and teaching effectiveness. How, they wondered, can you build in the nonverbal indicators with the technology?

Focus group participants discussed the importance of breaking through the impersonality of technology to cultivate a sense of caring and community—all concerns for the human issues related to technology. This concern was a key category identified by focus group faculty and identified by more than 80 percent of the survey respondents.

> On Wednesday of this week, I shall be teaching my first e-mail class. I worry about the lack of face-to-face (i.e., fully human) interaction.

> Technology can never replace the human need for warmth and compassion given by a caring teacher.

> Technology can actually get in the way of teaching and learning. You can rely on it so much you forget how your students are responding or reacting.

> Students and some instructors are fearful that the environment will become too depersonalized. Used inappropriately, technology can be cold and isolating.

> Technology should enhance the ability of faculty to draw students into the circle of learning. The most important factor in instruction is, I believe, the acting/exhibitionist piece of good teaching which catches the students and makes them yearn to hear/learn more. Technology shouldn't be in the way.

> In an ITV classroom, discussion is hard. It is stilted and shortened, and people don't "connect" to you or to each other in the same way.

> You lose the human element in some cases. I like the personal interaction with students, seeing their bright faces when something is clear and their blank stares when something isn't.

> Teaching emanates from love, which cannot be excluded from the process. Technology per se cannot build that special bridge between teacher and student that results from learning.

Conclusion

That "special bridge" must be strengthened in all teaching and learning relationships. We recognized a growing interest, woven throughout these shared perspectives, in putting technology to work in building these very special bridges in the future. These faculty spoke about balance and about using IT as an important collection of tools, one collection among many. And, they spoke in the support of reasoned discussion, to discovering pathways that could take us beyond the obvious shortcomings of the technology and toward making the best of the multiple opportunities the technology extends to us.

Some participants advised: "Be prepared! "Know what you're doing!" Others fretted: "There is so much to learn and so little time to learn it!" "I just can't bear to look as inept as

I feel!" Others put on a brave face and announced: "I owe it to myself; I owe it to my students." "I'm in there for the long haul. I've never let something like an enormous learning curve whip me yet!" In their responses, we saw ourselves, we saw their challenges, and we saw the community college tradition of responding to extraordinary circumstances.

The full power of the Chinese curse, "May you live in interesting times," will be determined in our collective futures by the responses that we make to the times in which we live. The thoughtfulness and the energy in the responses we gathered, and in the perceptions we described, challenge all of us to bring similar responses to the challenges of these interesting times.

Chapter Nine

Advice for Beginning Community College Instructors

Forget every stereotype about "college" or piece of conventional wisdom you've been given. And ignore—at least so far as providing a model for your own performance is concerned—what most of your own professors did in college. The point is not simply to replicate the stale process of past educational methodologies (to "pass the torch," as it were) but to create an environment in which students are encouraged to discover new fires for themselves! Yes, in most cases, it will still be the same old "fire," but to students who own *this knowledge and some awareness now of how they acquired it, it will be exciting and meaningful, and they will have the knowledge and enthusiasm to go on to share with others. Problems of lack of motivation fade away!*

—Evan Garrett, Schoolcraft College (MI)

There are no new ideas among the perspectives and advice that these award recipients offer to beginning community college instructors—just punctuation marks! The reader will find nothing surprising here. The perspectives from these award recipients are consistent to the end. Their advice to new faculty is drawn from their practice. It is practical magic explained—and at its best.

Responses to "What Advice Would You Give a Beginning Community College Instructor?"

Focus on Your Students

Your primary commitment is to students—keep your focus on that despite the fact that other things could consume your attention.

Don't be afraid to treat students individually. Artificial standards of "fairness" only apply to grading. Every student "gets it" in his own way.

Remember, you are the issue up front, not the content you've learned.

Your humanness is what's being learned.

See the individuals in your classes as "persons who have learning needs" versus "students who need to learn."

Learn students' names and then listen, listen, listen.

Love your students.

Learn about your students' interests.

Be compassionate, sensitive, and flexible. Community colleges are not the traditional higher education environments.

Care about students, even (or especially) when they don't seem to care.

Listen to your students' concerns—those spoken and those unspoken.

Be sure to make personal contact with students by setting office hours and encouraging conferences.

Find out who your students are, then go to meet them intellectually and lead them to the knowledge you have to share.

Talk to students and try to understand all the "stuff" they have going on in their lives!

The odds are against most of them!

NEVER allow a student to be disrespectful toward or make personal attacks against another.

Find out about your students; their backgrounds, and their experiences—then you can better determine how they "hear" you.

Care deeply about your students and communicate that you do. Students will often forgive an enormous number of your shortcomings if you just care about them.

Develop an atmosphere of trust so that students can relax and learn.

Understand that students have problems and interests that may be different from yours.

See each student as the unique and special individual that he or she is.

Your primary commitment is to students—keep your focus on that and less on all the other things that can consume your attention.

Enjoy students as "people."

Contact students by phone early in the term when they are absent—community college students need to feel "wanted."

It's important to remain "human" as a teacher. Don't get caught up in the institutional hierarchy of student, teacher, full professor, and the like.

Spend time finding out about each student IN CLASS so that they can experience the diversity represented by the students around them.

Put Forth the Effort Necessary to Be Effective

Work hard, go to class on time, go prepared, and stay the whole time!

Don't ever brag about what an easy job you have. Good teaching can be fun, passionate, and stimulating—but it's NEVER easy!

Don't expect or demand more of others than you do of yourself.

Develop a clear understanding of students' needs and collect the resources you must have to meet that need.

Teaching is tough work if you do it right.

Prepare MORE than your students!

Plan what your students will do in the classroom. What students remember most is what they've experienced and processed.

Be prepared for the dysfunctions in students' lives and anticipate how they will affect your teaching.

Being organized is a necessity for students who are committed to families, jobs, and other responsibilities outside the classroom. They need to know how to prepare and succeed.

To reduce tensions and calm your nerves, always enter the classroom prepared and organized; however, avoid being too rigid and making your *students* tense and nervous.

Find a method for organizing your material so that you can access it easily (e.g., file frequently in file drawers, organize your computer files for easy access).

Adult students are wonderful, but their complicated lives can really affect their work.

Especially in working with adult students, make sure your assignments are not "make work"—*nobody* has time for that!

Never go into a classroom unprepared. You better do your homework this time!

Be prepared, and be prepared to work HARD!

Find a Mentor

Participants in every focus group acknowledged that excellent mentors are *absolutely* essential—powerful words of advice!

Select a mentor who will *actively* help you understand how to grow as a teacher and thrive in the department and college—one who will encourage and challenge you to do your best.

Get to know an experienced teacher at the college, and spend time discussing how to FUNCTION in this place.

Be very clear; consult with others continually about WHAT you're teaching. Don't be a lone ranger!

Pick a good mentor and learn!

Find out who the *really* good teachers are, and ask if you can attend their classes.

Attend lectures of faculty who have received teaching excellence awards in the past.

A great mentor can pave the way; an apathetic, indifferent one serves no purpose.

Don't be afraid to ASK when you need help.

Watch the good instructors—learn from them!

Look around. Pick out faculty who enjoy teaching, and find out what they do.

Get to know the "doers" in the college—you don't need the "talkers."

Team teach with a mentor.

Listen openly to lots of advice, but understand that at some point you'll have to create your own system and style.

Steal all the good ideas you can find!

Find a great mentor, one who can share ideas, offer personal and professional support, and has your *respect* as a role model.

Find the professor with a "non-required" course whose classrooms fill up, and then OBSERVE, OBSERVE, OBSERVE!

Be Positive

Make your students think that teaching their class is the most fun you will have all day!

Always be positive—use positive comments and encourage students as much and as often as possible.

ATTITUDE is the key.

Try, try again!

Don't be afraid to "fail."

Remain positive and focused on why you are here. It's easy to blame the school system (K–12) for your students' shortcomings. Remember, the past is past. You are there to help them ALL succeed.

Be enthusiastic.

Have fun, and your students will, too.

Don't take yourself too seriously.

Take your subject—not yourself—seriously.

There will always be days, even after years of experience, where it just doesn't go right! Think of the "less than wonderful" as a humbling experience; then believe in yourself again, and get ready for the next cloud.

Be enthusiastic—show your passion, love your discipline, love your job, appreciate your students' abilities.

Keep a sense of humor—and realize that not everyone is as crazy, interested, frantic, and absorbed (in and about your disciplines) as you!

Don't be a turf-protector!

Always act like you're glad to be there.

Resist the temptation to become discouraged (or bitter) when some students simply do not respond to your care and concern.

Don't think of yourself as being inexperienced, but rather as the "latest model" with the newest innovations.

Remember that fear is the root of all student hostilities.

Don't "beat yourself up."

When students preface their questions with "This is a dumb question," tell them that only the unasked question is dumb. Tell them to ask!

Nourish their spirits—be positive!

Be able to laugh at yourself (and your mistakes).

Insist on having fun!

Get rid of your self-limiting thoughts and prejudices.

Don't feel that you are a second-rate teacher because you don't teach at a university.

Be a positive contributor to your college—be a part of solutions. Surround yourself with positive energy. It will help you cope with demands.

Don't "rag" on students, secretaries, staff, or administration. It's a contagious cancer!

Stay out of the teachers' lounge if it has an air of negativity toward other faculty, students, and the college!

Stay positive even when pressures or limited opportunities bring out the negative.

Avoid negative and cynical faculty like the plague—their sickness can destroy your work and your life.

Set High Standards for Yourself and Your Students

Hold your students to high standards, but encourage them along the way by building in opportunities for small successes.

Describe your standards "in print" beginning day one. Hand out two copies; have them sign one and return the other for your files.

Always display professional, ethical behavior—be a mentor/role model for your students.

Model the behavior you expect from students in your presentations to the class and your relationships with them.

Set high, reasonable standards; be demanding.

Be able to see the potential in all students.

Expect excellence, and encourage students to expect it of themselves.

Be clear and firm about your expectations from day one.

Expect the best from your students.

Don't ease the students into work. Set high standards at the outset; it will be far too difficult to set them later on.

Combine high expectations with the tools students need to be successful.

Caring behaviors are crucial to this job. But remember that you are expected to be the teacher and students the learners. Don't get too informal; it's not a situation of equals—and students don't want it to be.

I wouldn't say not to be "blown away" by the skill levels of community college students to the point of forgetting your standards. Set high standards and goals, and realize it's your job to help them get there.

Start at the student level, but do NOT compromise or lower your standards or expectations.

Don't "dumb down" your course.

Strive for—no, *insist on*—high standards with increasingly academically diverse students. This may be our greatest challenge, but students must be shown that good writing, good speaking, poise, presence, respectful behavior, and positive attitudes have always been benchmarks of an educated society.

You just give (assign) the grade—the student earns it; have guidelines and stick to them.

Just because most of your students will be working full time, don't even consider lowering your standards—you won't be doing them any favors.

Be Open and Honest

Tell the truth. There is nothing so deadly as trying to fake it.

Corollary #1: It's okay to say, "I don't know."

Corollary #2: It's not okay to say, "I don't know," and then not pursue the answer and have it ready when the class next meets.

Admit you don't know everything—enjoy learning with the students.

Be human and see students as human.

Don't be afraid to admit what you don't know.

It's "OK" not to know absolutely *everything*.

Tell stories about your own life—it will make you more human to your students.

Try to relax, be yourself, and don't try to impress students with your knowledge.

Tell students you are learning, too—and that they can help you learn.

Be yourself—they can spot a phony anytime.

Explore and Utilize a Range of Teaching Techniques

Take a course in teaching strategies if you have had no formal teaching/education experiences.

Don't be afraid to try something new!

Become a facilitator, not a lecturer.

Remember the "best" teacher(s) from whom you learned the most and adapt or emulate that teacher's style.

Look at what experienced, excellent teachers are doing, and make their behaviors your own.

Steal—yes, steal, if you must—good material and styles.

Remember that just when you think you've "got it," "it" won't work the next time!

Consider that your teaching style may not fit a student's learning style.

A lot of teachers don't begin as "stars," or even very good teachers, at first. You'll have to *learn* how to be one!

Teaching is a life long learning process—use your experience to improve every time you teach a course.

Continually try new "stuff."

Don't be afraid to try new approaches.

Start a journal. Be reflective. Acknowledge yourself as a novice.

Never stop learning/giving. You and your courses are works in progress.

Work toward progress, not perfection. There is no such thing.

Take chances—maybe not right away, but understand that some efforts/theories won't work out.

A great idea that took much effort to prepare may not go as you had hoped—don't allow this to deter you from stepping out and being creative in the future. Risk taking is a growing experience.

Be open to constructive criticism.

View yourself as a "knowledge navigator," but students as captains of their ships!

Teaching is great! I've had many jobs in the business world, but in teaching you get to start "fresh" each semester and put your inspirations from the last semester into practice. Try *this* in any other field!

Never be satisfied with what you are doing today!

Avoid the tendency to teach the way you were taught. It probably won't work anymore.

From time to time, surprise your students— try a new format, topic, or activity.

Be PATIENT—students frequently need more creative approaches to learning; they may be willing and eager (for the most part), but everything takes time.

Take time to talk with students about what works and what doesn't.

Don't change your teaching style to please others. Continue to develop your own— be open to ideas and suggestions.

Get over the idea that you know how to teach!

Continue to learn—you are not "finished" simply because you are employed.

Take classes in counseling techniques—learning how to respond in a non-intimidating way.

Take acting lessons!

Go to every workshop or professional development activity offered!

Read journals for new teaching ideas and instructional methods.

Go to conferences geared to two-year colleges in your discipline! Pick up on what's going on and where you need to be heading.

Try new "stuff," and know that you'll have a real clinker from time to time.

Don't reuse those old lesson plans. Build on them.

Lecturing is easy. Teaching is hard.

If you came from a four-year background, you'll find that the diversity of students' abilities, lives, and experiences is huge, and you need to find a way to use it constructively.

Trust your own instincts in the classroom; use instructional techniques that work for YOU, but be willing to experiment when students don't respond.

Get out from behind your desk or your podium.

Embrace the Notion of Teaching Life

Recognize that with proper motivation, modeling, and coaching, any student can be successful.

You don't just teach curriculum—you teach life.

Strive for Balance

"Keep cool, but don't freeze." (Advice given to matriculating freshmen at Harvard University by the president of Radcliffe College in 1982.)

Find a center, a physical or spiritual "place" you can return to whenever the stress gets too great.

Keep a balanced life. Don't let the college consume you. (It will try.)

Remain committed to your own growth and development, academically and personally.

Don't try to change the world in a day—give it a semester!

Set your priorities, and make sure that one task doesn't consume all of your time.

Take your subject matter seriously, but not yourself.

Keep an outside life alive—it is important to give yourself a balanced perspective.

Don't expect too much from yourself at first—teaching is extraordinarily time consuming, and you will probably feel overwhelmed. But it gets better every term.

Don't stay up all night preparing. It doesn't work well for students *or* teachers!

Take care of yourself—eat, sleep, laugh.

Don't try to be all things to all people—learn about your strengths, build on them; acknowledge your weaknesses, but don't dwell on them.

Don't tell students everything you know in 10 minutes.

Value Student Contributions

Never underestimate what students bring with them to the classroom.

Try new techniques and activities that involve students.

Get over being THE authority on all areas of your subject matter.

Do not pontificate from on high! Value your students' contributions.

Don't talk too much! Collectively, students are much more exciting and brilliant than you are alone.

Engage students in major decision-making activities, including creating the syllabi, deciding on the types of group activities, and helping design their exams.

Be Flexible

Be very flexible; that's a must.

Go for it! Have no limits! If it doesn't work, forgive yourself! Just remember to change it up the next time.

Be pragmatic.

Don't be a control freak

Value the Intrinsic Rewards

Don't expect to get RICH in the material way, but DO expect a GREAT and exciting life.

Help students develop confidence in themselves and taste some success. There is no better source of job satisfaction in the world!

Fall in love with your job; you have chosen the best profession in the world.

Be proud of your calling.

Don't be an "8 to 5'er" or a "clock watcher."

Determine to make a difference—definitely!

Honor and respect yourself. You're a teacher!

Love what you do, or don't do it!

Hold on—and enjoy the ride!

Have fun with the greatest profession in the world!

You will make a difference. Your students are the most appreciative people in the world—enjoy them!

When (if) it's no longer fun or your students become "bothers," get out.

Orient Yourself to the Community College Context and Your College

Learn about community college students right away!

Take part in multicultural experience workshops or sensitivity sessions.

Understand that community college students are not the same as university students.

Don't compare yourself to a university professor—absolutely not!

Ease students into the work—many have not been to school for 20 years or more; they are SCARED!

Make sure you really get to know your students the first day/week. They are very different from everything you think you know about the "typical" college student: They have to go to work, they may be married with children, they may be rebuilding their lives and will be insecure, and they live in a financial situation that makes paying $65 for a textbook almost entirely out of the question!

Learn to take students from where they are, not where you want or wish them to be.

Get to know people all over your campus—not just students and colleagues, but clerks, counselors, vending machine workers, groundskeepers, painters, secretaries, etc.

Be open to the diversity of age, race, background, goals, and preparedness in your college's student population.

Review the language and the focus of your college's mission/philosophy/objectives; compare them to your own. BE SURE THAT THEY ARE COMPATIBLE! Make this a great experience for you and the college!

Get Involved in College Activities

Attend as many school functions as you can possibly work into your schedule. Be a supporter! Know what's going on!

Respect the non-faculty staff and maintenance people. They can be tremendous assets.

Get involved in the entire college, not just your classroom.

Be involved in the community. Be involved on college committees.

Be good to the staff; they will be good to you.

Expect more of yourself than walking into a classroom, delivering the material, and leaving at the sound of the bell. You will be expected to participate in the life of the college—serve on committees, prepare for long hours, serve the community, and sincerely care for your students.

Get involved in the life of the college. Make it FUN for yourself and others.

Conclusion

> *Call it a clan, call it a network, call it a tribe, call it a family.*
> *Whatever you call it, whoever you are, you need one.*
> —Jane Howard

From our collective vantage points—via multiple years, varied assignments, shared experiences, and collegial relationships in the community college world, we can testify and confirm that the individuals who call these unique institutions their professional homes belong to a virtual family of believers and achievers. As citizens of this unique educational world, we share rituals, interests, challenges, literature, organizations, rewards, and celebrations—not unlike the citizens of any small town. We agree that these shared visions and energies strengthen the bonds—this community college world is, all things considered, still very small. And, it is not uncommon to hear the familiar phrase—the community college family.

Our experiences in conducting this study further affirmed our perceptions of community college people as family members; large groups of relative strangers filled focus session rooms, went to work on their tasks, talked together as if they had known each other forever, and—essentially—spoke the same language. That is not to say that there was overwhelming agreement on every issue, but the participants were genuinely engaged and informed; moreover, they agreed and disagreed on the particulars of various issues without losing sight of common goals—for example, improving teaching and learning, and creating climates and opportunities for student success.

We particularly enjoyed the moments just after each focus session ended and participants were leaving the room. Not *because* it was over, but because we basked in the "high" that their collective energies had created—and we relished the sights and sounds of multiple animated conversations among participants as they collected their materials and prepared to move on to other conference sessions. We hoped that friendships were being formed and networks were being established. It was a familial picture, we agreed. In fact, the next day one participant from an earlier focus session stopped by to tell us that he wished he had had the opportunity as a beginning community college instructor to sit in on such a moving, invigorating, information-filled session. In fact, he observed, he was going to take that idea home to his college and talk about offering a similar orientation activity every semester—and including *all* of the faculty! We are, all in this together. And what we are into, exactly, is enormous change.

> *Remember Joe College? The young man who after working hard in high school, arrived at Berkeley, where he set out to sample the rich and varied intellectual feast at the University of California. Joe was independent, self-motivated, and academically well prepared. About his junior year, Joe settled on a major field of study, which he pursued with diligence and increasing confidence in order to graduate in four years after his arrival.*
> —Schoch (1980, p. 1)

Schoch concluded, and we would all concur: "Joe doesn't live here anymore." However, *we do!* And if we live up to our own greatest expectations—and with a little help from our family and friends—today's Joe (and Jane) College could have a very bright future indeed.

Chapter Ten

Implications and Recommendations for Planning and Practicing Teaching Excellence

To work magic is to weave the unseen forces into form; to soar beyond sight; to explore the uncharted dream realm of the hidden reality.

—Starhawk (1979)

There is enormous power in magic, practical or not. The unknown quantity that creates the illusion of magic can be explained, so say professional magicians. However, in a real magic show, there is not much to be gained by explaining magic—certainly there are precious few rewards for the magician, and even fewer for the viewer. Once the elements of surprise and mystery are eliminated—that is, once we learn how, exactly, change happened and we could get a rabbit out of any hat—the excitement of the magic is diminished; we return to the ordinary, and we all are the poorer for it.

So perhaps there is an important place for impractical magic; it should be left for that impractical side of ourselves to enjoy. However, there is obviously another kind of magic—we have referred to it as practical, but it requires no less creativity, knowledge, planning, and disciplined practice than does the other. We believe, however, that there is much to be gained by explaining practical magic—the explanations will inform interested parties who can turn knowledge into action to improve the common good.

As with impractical magic, it is the skill of the performer that strengthens the illusion and intensifies the mystery; its quality rests on the magician's ability to make the activity appear easy, if not totally effortless. The NISOD Excellence Award recipients in this study made their practical magic look easy. As groups and as individuals, they spoke from experience and scholarship, from dedication and practice. The wisdom of their words informed our practice and can improve student learning; the message from their hearts will strengthen our resolve and our belief in the life and promise of practical magic. They are true artists!

> *To affect the quality of the day, that is the highest of arts.*
> —Henry David Thoreau

We are grateful to the colleges for recognizing these Excellence Award recipients and sharing them with us. Their perspectives provided us with an array of implications that led to recommendations for practice that we are privileged to share with others. The recommendations we offer are by no means extensive; they do not begin to address every issue or perspective that the participants shared. However, they should provide some rich discussion topics and some good ideas to test out in the foreseeable future. We offer them to all colleges that are committed to the improvement of student learning, who agree that they, their staff and faculty, and their students "have serious business together." The challenges of this serious business are extraordinary, but dedicated professionals in community colleges are proving that the strength and intelligence of their commitment are keys to progress, as surely as the ultimate key to student success is the teacher in the classroom.

Celebrate the Power of Making a Difference

Change is often thrust upon us at what seems like inopportune times—when things are going along just fine, when we'd just as soon not have to change, or when we don't have enough money to change. That is how many people in higher education feel. But there are those among us who have caught a sense of what these changes can mean. We have the opportunity to educate students for whom the college experience can be a life-altering one. It is a time when our work in higher education can really and truly make a difference. (Upcraft, 1996, p. 3)

Making a difference in the lives of others was the overarching purpose for their own lives as teachers, according to the award recipients. According to Erikson (1950), this is a natural phenomenon, occurring in later stages of human development when individuals become more concerned with the welfare of future generations. This concern has been referred to as *generativity*—"a desire to invest one's substance in forms of life and work that will outlive the self" (Kotre, 1984, p. 10). As for teachers, evidence suggests that the more years they remain in the classroom, the more interested they become in improving their skills and staying in touch with their former students (Baldwin & Blackburn, 1981; Lawrence & Blackburn, 1985).

Professional development specialists indicate that research findings support their paying more attention to helping educators improve their interpersonal and social skills—for example, assisting faculty in designing collaborative learning situations, involving them in more extracurricular activities with students and advising roles, encouraging them to teach more courses in sequence to see their students develop, and establishing mentoring programs whereby more experienced faculty partner with younger or more novice faculty and share their knowledge and experiences (Walker & Quinn, 1996).

Participants told us about teachers who became their role models or who encouraged them to put their own talents to work in their own classrooms in the future. They credited them with their decision to become teachers, too. Many such influential teachers may have never known the enormous effect they had on another's life. The power to do good—to make a difference in and out of the classroom—is overwhelming.

So is the power to entice others who might be exceptional teachers of the future. We are reminded of a ritual at Richland College, conducted monthly, during which a small group of celebrants exit the president's office, armed with noisemakers, cheering and shouting for others to join them. As they wind their way around the campus, others take part in the familiar ritual—a long parade of celebrants making their way to the office or the desk of the "employee of the month." No one but the president knows the destination and identity of the honoree, but the group finally arrives at its destination; a great cheer goes up, and the applause is deafening! Do students enjoy watching this parade? If this is their first time to experience the community of celebrants honoring one of their own, they are probably shocked and amazed! We suspect most students—and, most likely, a good number of educators—are surprised by such a demonstration; that is a regrettable suspicion, but probably accurate.

All students need to be so inspired by positive behaviors that could make being in a positive community of learners especially attractive and inviting. We recommend celebrations on college campuses—as much for the individuals being honored as for the indelible, positive impressions they can make on students. Education, as one colleague observed, should not be "grim and serious business."

It would be particularly ironic to find grim, serious, arrogant artifices in what we often call democracy's college. We are all a part of a movement toward making a difference in the lives of students and communities. And given the educational, political, social, economic, and technological trends outlined here and in myriad other reports, there has never been such "a time for the community college" (Milliron, 2002a, 2002b; Milliron & de los Santos,

2002; Roueche et al., 2001; Roueche & Roueche, 1999). It should not be surprising then, that we ardently echo the idealism and commitment of the faculty members who participated in this study. They truly celebrated being a part of a community college and relished the mission of our institutions.

Encourage and Support Proactive Interest in the Scholarship of Teaching and Learning

> [A] consideration of how professors learn to teach can be greatly informed by reflecting on what and how professors continue to learn about other things. The writing of a book is one way, for it may well force the professor into mastering at least an elementary knowledge of many disciplines. Like the sculptor who must learn to be a welder or metallurgist or master mason or geologist, professors who attempt a large understanding of a complex subject may have to acquire many skills. Similarly, a great deal of disparate learning takes place as a result of the demands teaching places upon teachers. (Eble, 1983, p. 137)

One of the enormous benefits of taking on a research project like this one is that we are compelled to read, read, and read some more about what others are saying about the subjects addressed in our research activities. We agreed that, without a submission deadline looming in the near future, we could just curl up and read our days away. We would be likely to re-read any number of older books and reports that we may not have appreciated as much in the past as we appreciate now. For example, we experienced a renewed appreciation of the basic truths about a wide range of traditional teaching strategies (including discussion and lecture), all wrapped in the good wit that Eble brought to *The Craft of Teaching* (1976); we laughed out loud! And we welcomed the straightforward and reader-friendly discussions of complex subjects such as what cognitive scientists can tell us about how to improve learning, as Patricia Cross laid out in *Learning Is About Making Connections* (1999).

These examples are but two of so many just in the tip of our resource iceberg, but they are among our favorites. It is difficult to convince many others that "curling up in front of a good fire with a good book on teaching" can rate high on one's list of favorite things to do, but we experienced that. Moreover, we think that encouraging faculty, administrators, and staff to share their favorite sources and lessons is a compelling practice. It is seriously "good talk about good teaching" (Palmer, 1993, p. 8).

By way of example, one of us (Suanne Roueche) has fond memories of a community college department chair who encouraged her charges to stay current with practice by clipping articles and placing them in our mailboxes. She never believed that she was chiding us for some poor performance; she always attached a kindly worded, handwritten note, something on the order of "Thought you might enjoy reading this; I did" or "I thought about your question of last week, and I wonder if you might find this useful." Moreover, she shared announcements about upcoming events—such as musical performances or classic films coming to town. She was "educating the whole person."

At the time, most of us in the department were young and inexperienced enough that we probably missed most of the points she was making—we did not realize the depth of her engagement with our work or the favor she was doing us by encouraging the development of scholarship or the interest she was taking in our personal and professional growth and development. No doubt, she honestly wanted to pass along helpful information and interesting ideas. Her "clip and share" technique eventually became a permanent addition to at least one young teacher's collection of professional development activities.

Not only did this technique turn into a lifelong habit, it reinforced an important learning principle that was subject for discussion in literally every focus group session. These award recipients viewed their students holistically; they assumed the responsibility of teaching their subject within the larger real-world context. They spoke to the learning principles of making connections and building minds—helping students construct a schemata for learning. That is, they understood well that "you gotta know somethun' to learn somethun'" (cited in Sticht & McDonald, 1989, p. 31). We were reminded by the renowned reading specialist, Chall (1983) that the more "world information" we have, the better we can process new information in any medium and the more structures we can create to "re-structure" or fine-tune the information we have. Adelman expanded on this concept:

> The more "world information" you possess, for example, the more you can laugh at the allusive banter of late night television hosts such as Arsenio Hall or David Letterman, or a deft film script such as Steve Martin's *L.A. Story*. This is not a new story. Humor is a product of empowerment and enriches the life of any society. When we laugh together, we are less likely to confront each other in anger. People who know nothing from Shakespeare laugh less at a showing of *L.A. Story* than people who do. Comparatively and figuratively speaking, the space of their lives is a smidgen smaller. The point remains the same even when one changes the movie and its allusions. And it remains the same if one changes the culture and the language of the move and its allusions. (Adelman, 1992, p. 8)

Our participants observed that the more they engaged in their own learning, in and out of their disciplines, the more convinced they were to weave together extracurricular learning in and out of the classroom for their students. With that thought in mind, we propose that faculty regularly enroll in courses at the college, taught by faculty members they admire, first to help them recall what being a student is all about, and second to reinforce some of the critical aspects of student learning—for example, the relationships between present learning and new learning—a complex matter, indeed. Moreover, as new techniques and technologies for learning emerge, experiencing these from the perspective of learner is always a more meaningful experience than reading reports, seeing demonstrations, or reviewing outcome measures (Milliron, 2002b).

Finally, we offer two of Eble's insightful observations about student learning, drawn directly from his struggles with learning a foreign language in an organized French class. They provide powerful summations of our participants' perspectives on perfecting their craft, generally, and their teaching abilities, specifically. These observations underscore the critical need to really "know" students and how they approach their own learning, and the responsibility to "create climates" to promote improved learning.

I learned how much my students' learning is inhibited by their not wanting to make mistakes, dodging what is difficult for them, following the paths of other interests or less resistant learning. Even now, I am talking about learning from this experience…the learning of something about teaching, which is congenial and comfortable…I had to revive my past respect for exceptional…teachers I have had.…

Our work as teachers cannot count on the vitality of the subject itself nor the impulses of the student to learn nor a reinforcing context in the culture. We must provide assistance both to overcome the students' own internal impediments to learning and to increase the willingness of the student to work at this particular kind of learning. (Eble, 1983, p. 140)

Bring the Best Thinking to a Discussion of Information Technology Use

Consider carefully the upsides of the technology (and the downsides to the college, faculty, and students), how it will improve learning (or not), and how it will strengthen (or weaken) the academic community the college has established. Technology is an expensive budget item. Seriousness must prevail about the cost, the value, and the outcomes of using IT in instruction. Sources of information about how other colleges are responding to these questions and their inherent challenges are easy to come by and are "must reads." Obviously, every college must make its decisions based on its current situation. However, we make some recommendations here, based on the findings of this study. We believe that they should be subjects of discussion and offer them up as worthy of serious consideration.

We recommend that colleges investigate the current uses of technology across their curriculum. Students should have access to at least the minimum amount of technology necessary to produce their work and learn how to learn. They should learn how to use the technology that will allow them to develop competencies in word processing, at least, and preferably with presentation software and spreadsheets. They should be provided e-mail accounts and Internet access. The skills students should develop with this technology currently are considered the minimum requirements for keeping all students on a reasonably equal educational footing.

Colleges must work toward expanding access to asynchronous, technology-enabled learning options, such as Web tutorials and computer-based training, to allow students to make progress at their own pace. Faculty should have access to software, hardware, and training to improve their presentation skills and products; faculty observed that visual presentation technologies can "bring instruction to life." They should include technology applications in instruction that increase and improve communication between and among faculty, students, and college personnel-at-large. Especially useful for part-time students, as well as for part-time faculty, e-mail accounts can greatly enhance connectivity at all levels. And, believe it or not, even in 2003, e-mail remains the "killer application" of the Internet—chiefly because of its ability to connect those in the learning process.

Faculty should encourage students to use the Internet and other technology-based research tools in instruction, build curricula that encourage students to access research materials using technology, and use the technology themselves to facilitate their own learning in their disciplines and fields. Faculty should also concentrate on using technology to better manage their courses and improve assessment record keeping.

Colleges must think strategically about how to provide increased technology access and technical support, in particular, to students, faculty, and staff who do not have access anywhere other than at the college. Moreover, they should consider ways to provide additional access opportunities at the college. The majority of study participants described student access to computers in college computer labs; a large number of them described some new roles that are developing for librarians in the college library. For example, one librarian described the current situation at her college as follows: "In the library, we're no longer just information providers, we're tool providers, as well. We don't just have a reference desk, we have to have a service desk, too."

Students need information, but they also need to know how to access it—that is, use the technology. Many agreed that libraries are the places to which more and more students, and faculty, will look for expanded access to technology. They reported that students are coming into college libraries in record numbers and requesting help with what are essentially non-library functions, such as registration or applying for financial aid. Technology is changing the face of the college library.

Participants told us that IT literacy is the new basic skill. Colleges should require IT literacy components in programs and courses; students should have to demonstrate competency in these skills and should be encouraged to use the technology in their own learning. Moreover, faculty hiring practices and procedures for evaluating them should include a technology literacy component as well.

As we expect faculty to prepare students for their examinations, faculty should expect their colleges to provide adequate training and time-on-task to bring faculty up-to-speed; make use of the technology to bring others to the table—catalog and showcase the ways that instructors are using technology to improve their own instruction; feature model instructional uses on a regular basis; use professional development activities to encourage sharing experiences in technology applications; and develop mentoring arrangements whereby faculty who are further down the IT highway can provide instruction and support for others not so advanced. We recall participants emphasizing the critical role that technology can play when it is *used well*.

Discussions about using technology in college will include the inevitable disagreements about what technology tools are absolutely essential and how much the college can afford. Arguments to be avoided are those that include the idea that "it will save us money in the long run"—the expenses associated with technology's installation and ongoing applications must be considered logically and rationally with college goals in mind. The question is no longer whether or not technology should be applied to instruction; the questions are how, how much, and to what ends. Arguments on both sides of any issue can be valid; moreover, intelligent critics should be on both sides of every issue.

One of the arguments our participants identified was that sometimes "that stuff just doesn't work." When that happens, the college should have some surefire strategies for responding promptly to breakdowns and should require faculty to have contingency plans. Infrastructures to provide support for technology are expensive. The array of questions about the distances colleges and individuals must travel to get from "wow" to the "how" of making technology useful (Roueche & Roueche, 2001), about the seductive nature of distance learning that lures as many students who are unprepared to handle the responsibilities and the realities of this method of learning as it lures students who are more advanced (although the failure rate suggests we are not there yet with this delivery system; Roueche & Roueche, 2002), and about the time and cost of up-front instruction to prepare students (and faculty) to use even the most basic technology are serious issues that must be addressed. If the technology does not contribute to or measurably enhance instruction, it is not necessary. If it does not work properly or if it works erratically, it is an enormous distraction and a potential disaster.

Finally, participants warned that for all of the positive and exciting aspects of IT, it can never replace the human element. Learning communities may include the technology, but they must include the human, for at least two reasons that immediately come to mind. One is that experience tells us that "high-tech, high-touch" is an extraordinary concept. Although the presence of a real person on the other end of the line may reduce the isolation and distance that technology can create, the activity remains "lonely," and especially if that situation never changes. The second reason is that technology can never replace the human mind's ability to anticipate and respond to the environment. Bruce Schneier (a prominent creator of codes and ciphers; author of the classic, *Applied Cryptography,* and co-founder of Counterpane Internet Security, after abandoning cryptography in 1999) reported that, in helping governments and companies keep their secrets secret, his company is "dedicated to bringing one of the oldest forms of policing—the cop on the beat—to the digital realm" (cited in Mann, 2002, p. 86). An observation he made about the importance of always including the human component in a technical system, no matter how sophisticated the technology, is equally applicable here:

> Highly trained…these people brought to the task a quality not yet found in any technology: human judgment, which is at the heart of most good security. Human beings do make mistakes, of course. But they can recover from failure in ways that machines and software cannot. The well-trained mind is ductile. It can understand surprises and overcome them. (cited in Mann, 2002, p. 102)

Assess Student Learning Purposefully, Systematically, and in a Timely Way

> *Honest criticism is hard to take, particularly from a relative, a friend, an acquaintance,*
> *or a stranger.*
> —Franklin P. Jones (cited in McWilliams, 1995, p. 152)

Some findings of research on teaching indicate that although faculty typically have sought feedback, they

> seem more inclined to focus on the feedback itself (its veracity, relevance, and what the institution might do with it) than on the changes it might call for.…
>
> Part of the reluctance to deal with feedback is that often it identifies or relates to some problematic aspect of instruction.…Instructional problems

are not something most faculty are disposed to consider thoughtfully or discuss with others…It is much safer and easier for faculty to talk about improving student learning than about improving their teaching. (Menges et al., 1996, p. 150)

Commitment to improvement and success requires an enormous curiosity about what works and the courage to leave behind what does not. We were reminded by the participants that, among other things, raising the bar on oneself by benchmarking practices and outcomes against successful others carries high risk, psychologically, that may be painful to professional psyches but absolutely essential for improvement. Using classroom research strategies to stay informed about the quality of students' learning on a daily basis is critical to improvement and goes a long way to assure students that instructors care about students' success. However, participants essentially agreed with findings from other research that the problem with identifying best practices and labeling some better than others is that, all in all, it appears that "different methods seem to end up pretty much equal…there are circumstances and conditions under which most instructional methods do and don't work" (Menges et al., 1996, p. 151). The willingness to make changes on their side of the desk is fundamental to making enormous changes on the other.

Finally, share that commitment to assessment as an institutionwide focus on measuring effectiveness. Colleges should commit to achieving quality results and sharing evidence with the larger community, in and out of the institution. Colleges are also well advised to create units within themselves to regularly discuss, plan, promote, and support the improvement of student performance. Just as departments and programs can inform institutionwide pursuits of excellence, annual planning cycles can help colleges monitor progress toward effectiveness goals, similar to the monitoring procedures currently being implemented at the Community College of Denver, which we discussed in an earlier chapter.

Recognize and Reward Excellence

A sobering thought: what if, right at this very moment, I am living up to my full potential?
—Jane Wagner

We do not know how often accomplished professionals ask themselves this question, but it is worth some consideration. Striving to become a better person, teacher, or parent is a phenomenon that most of us would agree is built into the psyches of the majority of rational individuals—and certainly in the minds of anyone who respects and values personal and professional involvement in lifelong learning. However, it is clear that living up to one's full potential is situation- and individual-specific. There are talents that some of us simply may never want to develop further, and so we are quite comfortable with having reached our full potential! There are others that we are drawn to out of need or curiosity, and we keep plugging away at improving our performance or learning all we can.

Colleges recognizing and rewarding excellence report that one of the characteristics common among the individuals they identify is that they simply are never totally satisfied with the number or level of their achievements—they are proud of their accomplishments, but not satisfied that they have reached all of their goals. They also report that recognizing stellar performance sends a message to everyone at the college that excellence is valued by the institution. The value and strength of the recognition process, according to our participants, was that the college had given careful thought to the criteria that would be applied to all nominations; that is, the college had considered its expectations and had put those expectations in writing. Many participants observed that although the culture of their colleges supported a collective institutional responsibility for achieving student success goals, everyone understood and accepted individual responsibilities as well.

> Teachers teach, students learn, in bad weather as well as good. Some measures can be taken…that might increase recognition of teaching, both its visibility and in rewards….Teaching comes into prominence to some degree as departments, colleges, and universities examine their criteria for good teaching, their procedures for reviewing it, and their stated expectations with regard to faculty performance. Such examination is necessary if reward is to follow recognition and if a college community as a whole is to perceive the high place of teaching in the reward structure. (Eble, 1970, pp. 5–6)

Our participants observed that they would work toward excellence with or without reward or recognition. Most reported, as did researchers, that teachers testified that intrinsic rewards were significant reinforcement and, in the majority of cases, were the impetus for stellar performance. However, we made two observations during our sessions that we thought worthy of further discussion. One, recognizing excellence brings everyone's attention to "moments of truth." As the president of SAS Airlines, Jan Carlzon, once observed:

> Last year, each of our 10 million customers came in contact with approximately five SAS employees, and this contact lasted an average of 15 seconds each time. Thus, SAS is "created" 50 million times a year, 15 seconds at a time. These 50 million "moments of truth" are the moments that ultimately determine whether SAS will succeed or fail as a company. They are the moments when we must prove to our customers that SAS is their best alternative. (Carlzon, 1987, p. 3)

Two, colleges must prove themselves every day. We have learned that you can do almost everything right, and just one wrong thing can be disastrous. Just as teachers are walking billboards for their noble profession, their students are walking billboards for the college. The hope is that their version of what is passed on to others is the story that the college wants to tell.

> A satisfied customer is like a walking billboard….By exceeding peoples' expectations you make a statement—their needs come first. All of us feel good when something like that happens in our lives. It's such a contrast to the every day grind of broken promises, late deliveries, surly secretaries, and unreturned telephone calls. Imagine what would happen if a college…began to exceed the expectations of its customer—employers, students, alumni, parents, board

members, state legislators, local community members. Imagine the stories that would be told and retold. (Seymour, 1993, p. 179)

Conclusion

As this study progressed, we began to key in on words and phrases that frequently appeared in survey responses, in focus group conversations, and thus in the transcripts of focus group discussions. Eventually, they began to jump off the page. We conclude this report with two examples: *nobility of teaching* and *hope*.

> *Get this right. Teaching our students is a noble profession, and we need to pass that feeling on.*
> —NISOD Excellence Award recipient and focus group participant

A seasoned community college teacher stared deep into our eyes and delivered this admonition as the final focus group concluded and participants made their way out of the room. He held the stare long enough to make it clear that he was serious. That moment has stayed with us: It captured the spirit of common purpose, the unique styles, and the sense of a higher calling both described and demonstrated by the faculty we studied.

We were particularly pressed to conduct this study given the increasing demands for improved performance at all levels of education—especially in institutions of higher education. And, after also taking into account the serious concerns about the projected massive turnover of faculty nationwide, the flood of reform movements, increasing numbers of competitors in the education market, and rampant, often unchallenged, admonitions about the changing nature of learning, it seemed particularly important to listen to professionals on the front lines of teaching and learning. We were not disappointed with what we heard—their insights deftly cut through the hyperbole to useful day-to-day strategies that really make a difference with students.

> *Why did I become a teacher?—the hope that I can make a difference in someone's life.*
> —NISOD Excellence Award recipient

Our experiences support our beliefs that anything is possible in community colleges! We believe that they are America's best hope for positive change. We leave this subject knowing full well that community colleges will always have their critics—and that positive, constructive criticism is always welcome. Ultimately, we were reminded of an observation, made more than a decade ago, by Steven Zwerling (1976), author of *Second Best*—arguably one of the most critical indictments ever of community colleges. Shortly after Miami-Dade Community College (FL) had been recognized as the top teaching college in America (in a 1985 independent survey), skeptic Zwerling visited its four campuses to investigate exactly what that college had accomplished to have been so honored. He observed:

> My basic views about the community college movement had not shifted. Yes, Miami-Dade and a few outposts of excellence did exist about the country, but from my research and visits to dozens of other two-year colleges, I was still

convinced that most places were in fact too often *mis*-serving their students' potential. I came finally to feel, ironically, the Miami-Dade experience had reinforced my view that something was fundamentally wrong at our urban two-year colleges—especially if a place as large and diverse as Miami was able to accomplish so much. It seemed essential that what I had learned and what it could teach should be even more widely known. There was still certainly enough for despair, but there was also more reason to *hope*. (1988, p. 23)

> *"Hope" is the thing with feathers—that perches in the soul.*
> —Emily Dickinson

Hope has always been a hallmark in our American celebrations; it was in the heart and soul of the literature we revisited for this report. We revisited it in Page Smith's tribute to community college faculty as the "hope of higher education in America" (1990, pp. 19–20), in Zwerling's "more reason to hope" for positive change, and in the AACU National Panel report, *Greater Expectations:*

> Hope is on the horizon…despite…barriers to readiness and quality…and it comes from three directions:
> - first, from the recognized past successes of U.S. higher education in serving the college-going population and society;
> - second, from recent great accomplishments in opening the doors of college to many more who wish to attend;
> - third, from the new creativity…as faculty members across the country reinvent their own institutions' practices for a contemporary education.
> These innovators' dedication to students, to more integrated forms of learning, and to the *noble profession of college teaching* are already producing effective educational models that, taken together, provide a glimpse of the future—of a universal college education of high quality for the twenty-first century. (AACU, 2002, p. 19)

It was no surprise to us that hope bubbled up in our transcripts. We celebrate the award recipients who shared it, brought it to life by their presence, made this study possible and worthwhile, and ultimately make a difference every day. It is with a renewed sense of hope for us all that we close.

References

Abrami, P. C. (1985). Dimensions of effective college instruction. *Review of Higher Education, 8*, 211–228.

Adelman, C. (1992). *Tourists in our own land: Cultural literacies and the college curriculum.* Washington, DC: U.S. Department of Education.

Aleamoni, L. M. (1987). Typical faculty concerns about student evaluation of teaching. In L. M. Aleamoni (Ed.), *New directions for teaching and learning: No. 31. Techniques for evaluating and improving instruction.* San Francisco: Jossey-Bass.

Alfred, R. L. (1994). Measuring teaching effectiveness. In T. O'Banion (Ed.), *Teaching and learning in the community college* (pp. 263–283). Washington, DC: Community College Press.

American Psychological Association. (1997). *Learner-centered psychological principles: A framework for school redesign and reform.* Washington, DC: Author.

Anandam, K. (1989). Expanding horizons for learning and technology. In T. O'Banion (Ed.), *Innovation in the community college* (pp. 98–112). New York: ACE/Macmillan.

Andrews, H. A. (1995). *Teachers can be fired! The quest for quality.* Chicago: Catfeet Press.

Angelo, T. A. (1993). A "teacher's dozen": Fourteen general, research-based principles for improving higher education in our classrooms. *American Association for Higher Education Bulletin, 45*(8), 3–7.

Angelo, T. A. (1996). Relating exemplary teaching to student learning. In M. Svinicki & R. J. Menges (Eds.), *New directions for teaching and learning: No. 65. Honoring exemplary teaching* (pp. 57–64). San Francisco: Jossey-Bass.

Angelo, T. A., & Cross, K. P. (1993). *Classroom assessment techniques: A handbook for college teachers* (2nd ed.). San Francisco: Jossey-Bass.

Arreola, R. A. (1995). *Developing a comprehensive faculty evaluation system.* Bolton, MA: Anker.

Association of American Colleges and Universities. (2002). *Greater expectations: A new vision for learning as a nation goes to college* (National Panel Report). Washington, DC: Author.

Astin, A. W. (1985). *Achieving education excellence: A critical assessment of priorities and practices in higher education.* San Francisco: Jossey-Bass.

Axelrod, J. (1970). Teaching styles in the humanities. In W. H. Morris (Ed.), *Effective college teaching* (pp. 38–55). Washington, DC: American Association for Higher Education.

Baker, G. A. III, Roueche, J. E., & Gillett-Karam, R. (1990). *Teaching as leading: Profiles of excellence in the open-door college.* Washington, DC: Community College Press.

Baldwin, R. G., & Blackburn, R. T. (1981). The academic career as a developmental process: Implications for higher education. *Journal of Higher Education, 52*, 26.

Banta, T. W. (1996). Using assessment to improve instruction. In R. J. Menges, M. Weimer, & Associates (Eds.), *Teaching on solid ground* (pp. 363–384). San Francisco: Jossey-Bass.

Barr, R. B. (1995). From teaching to learning: A new reality for community colleges. *Leadership Abstracts, 8*(3).

Barr, R. B., & Tagg, J. (1995). From teaching to learning: A new paradigm for undergraduate education. *Change, 27*(6), 13–25.

Barsi, L. M. (1991). Some illustrative vignettes on the uses of the seven principles and the faculty and institutional inventories. In A. W. Chickering & Z. F. Gamson (Eds.), *New directions for teaching and learning: No. 47. Applying the seven principles of good practice in undergraduate education* (pp. 37–49). San Francisco: Jossey-Bass.

Bell, T. H. (1991). Technology in education in the nineties. *Leadership Abstracts, 4*(7).

Bergquist, W. H. (1995). *Quality through access, access with quality: The new imperative for higher education.* San Francisco: Jossey-Bass.

Bloom, A. D. (1956). *Taxonomy of educational objectives: Handbook I. Cognitive domain.* New York: David McKay.

Bloom, A. D. (1980). The new direction in educational research: Alterable variables. *Phi Delta Kappan, 61,* 382–385.

Bloom, A. D. (1987). *The closing of the American mind.* New York: Simon & Schuster.

Boggs, G. R. (1993). Community colleges and the new paradigm. *Celebrations.* Austin, TX: National Institute for Staff and Organizational Development.

Boggs, G. R. (1996). The learning paradigm. *Community College Journal, 66*(3), 24–27.

Boice, R. (1991). New faculty as teachers. *Journal of Higher Education, 62*(2), 150–173.

Boone, E. J. (1997). National perspective of community colleges. *Community College Journal of Research and Practice, 21,* 1–12.

Boyer, E. L. (1987). *The undergraduate experience in America.* New York: HarperCollins.

Boyer, E. L. (1990). *Scholarship reconsidered: Priorities of the professoriate.* Princeton, NJ: Carnegie Foundation for the Advancement of Teaching.

Brassard, M. (1989). *The memory jogger plus+: Seven management and planning tools.* Methuen, MA: Goal/QPC.

Brookfield, S. D. (1986). *Understanding and facilitating adult learning: A comprehensive analysis of principles and effective practices.* San Francisco: Jossey-Bass.

Brookfield, S. D. (1990). *The skillful teacher: On technique, trust and responsiveness in the classroom.* San Francisco: Jossey-Bass.

Brookfield, S. D. (1994). Adult learners: Motives for learning and implications for practice. In K. A. Feldman & M. B. Paulsen (Eds.), *Teaching and learning in the college classroom* (pp. 137–49). Needham Heights, MA: Ginn Press.

Brown, G., & Atkins, M. (1988). *Effective teaching in higher education.* New York: Methuen.

Brown, J. W., & Thornton, J. W. (1963). *College teaching: Perspectives and guidelines.* New York: McGraw-Hill.

Business-Higher Education Forum. (1999). *Spanning the chasm: A blueprint for action.* Washington, DC: Author. Available from www.ace.nche.edu.

Carlzon, J. (1987). *Moments of truth.* New York: Harper & Row.

Carnevale, A. P. (2000). *Help wanted…College required.* Leadership Series. Princeton, NJ: Educational Testing Service.

Carnevale, A. P., & Fry, R. A. (2001). Economics, demography and the future of higher education policy. *Higher expectations: Essays on the future of postsecondary education.* Washington, DC: National Governors Association.

Centra, J. A. (1996). Identifying exemplary teachers: Evidence from colleagues, administrators, and alumni. In M. Svinicki & R. J. Menges (Eds.), *New directions for teaching and learning: No. 65. Honoring exemplary teaching* (pp. 51–56). San Francisco: Jossey-Bass.

Chall, J. S. (1983). *Stages of reading development.* New York: McGraw-Hill.

Chapman, B. (2001). Connecting instructional programs to fundraising [Abstract]. *Innovation Abstracts, 23*(23).

Chickering, A. W., & Gamson, Z. F. (1987). Seven principles for good practice in under-graduate education. *AAHE Bulletin, 39*(7), 3–7.

Chronicle of Higher Education. Almanac Issue 2001–2. August 31.

Cole, C. C., Jr. (1982). *Improving instruction: Issues and alternatives for higher education.* AAHE-ERIC/Higher Education Research Report No. 4. Washington, DC: American Association for Higher Education.

Community College Roundtable. (1994). *Community colleges: Core indicators of effectiveness.* Washington, DC: American Association of Community Colleges.

Coné, J. (2001). Lessons learned in the transition to technology-enabled learning. *Celebrations.* Austin, TX: National Institute for Staff and Organizational Development.

Cranton, P. (1994). Self-directed and transformational instructional development. *Journal of Higher Education, 65*(6), 726–744.

Cross, K. P. (1981). *Adults as learners.* San Francisco: Jossey-Bass.

Cross, K. P. (1994). Teaching to improve learning. In K. A. Feldman & M. B. Paulsen (Eds.), *Teaching and learning in the college classroom* (pp. 683–692). Needham Heights, MA: Ginn Press.

Cross, K. P. (1998). *Opening windows on learning.* Paper #2. Mission Viejo, CA: League for Innovation in the Community College.

Cross, K. P. (1999). *Learning is about making connections.* Mission Viejo, CA: League for Innovation in the Community College and Educational Testing Service.

Cross, K. P. (2000). *Collaborative learning 101.* The Cross Papers No. 4. Mission Viejo, CA: League for Innovation Press.

Cross, K. P. (2002). *The role of class discussion in the learning centered classroom.* Paper #6, ISBN 1-931300-32-1.

Cross, K. P., & Angelo, T. A. (1988). *Classroom assessment techniques: A handbook for faculty.* Ann Arbor, MI: National Center for Research to Improve Postsecondary Teaching and Learning.

Csikszentmihalyi, M. (1997). Intrinsic motivation and effective teaching: A flow analysis. In J. L. Bess (Ed.), *Teaching well and liking it: Motivating faculty to teach effectively* (pp. 73–89). Baltimore, MD: The Johns Hopkins University Press.

Daly, W. T. (1994). Teaching and scholarship: Adapting American higher education to hard times. *Journal of Higher Education, 65*(1), 45–58.

Davis, S. F. (1976). *Teaching strategies for the classroom.* Boulder, CO: Westview Press.

de los Santos, G. E., de los Santos, A. G., Jr., & Milliron, M. D. (2000). Community colleges bridge the digital divide. *Leadership Abstracts, 13*(1).

de los Santos, G. E., de los Santos, A. G., Jr., & Milliron, M. D. (2001). *Access in the information age: Community colleges bridging the digital divide.* Mission Viejo, CA: League for Innovation in the Community College.

D'Souza, D. (1991). *Illiberal education: The politics of race and sex on campus.* New York: The Free Press.

Duffy, D. K., & Jones, J. W. (1995). *Teaching within the rhythms of the semester.* San Francisco: Jossey-Bass.

Eble, K. E. (1970). *Recognition and evaluation of teaching.*

Eble, K. E. (1972). *Professors as teachers.* San Francisco: Jossey-Bass.

Eble, K. E. (1976). *The craft of teaching: A guide to mastering the professor's art.* San Francisco: Jossey-Bass.

Eble, K. E. (1983). *The aims of college teaching.* San Francisco: Jossey-Bass.

Education Trust. (1999). Ticket to nowhere. *Thinking K–16, 3*(2), 8.

Education Trust-West. (2002, April). *The high school diploma: Making it more than an empty promise.* Prepared for Senate Standing Committee on Education hearing on Senate Bill 1731.

Ellner, C. L., & Barnes, C. P. (1983). *Studies of college teaching: Experimental results, theoretical interpretations, and new perspectives.* Lexington, MA: Heath.

Elsner, P. A. (2001). Convening our partners. *Community College Journal, 71*(6), 18–23.

Erikson, E. H. (1950). *Childhood and society.* New York: Norton.

Evertson, C. M., & Green, J. L. (1986). Observations as inquiry and method. In M. C. Wittrock (Ed.), *Handbook of research on teaching* (3rd ed., pp. 162–163). New York: Macmillan.

Ewell, P. T. (1994). The assessment movement: Implications for teaching and learning. In T. O'Banion (Ed.), *Teaching and learning in the community college* (pp. 73–96). Washington, DC: Community College Press.

Feldman, K. A. (1976). The superior college teacher from the students' view. *Research in Higher Education, 5*, 243–259.

Feldman, K. A. (1988). Effective college teaching from the students' and faculty's view: Matched or mismatched priorities? *Research in Higher Education, 28*, 291–344.

Feldman, K. A. (1996). Identifying exemplary teaching: Using data from course and teacher evaluations. In M. Svinicki & R. J. Menges (Eds.), *New directions for teaching and learning: No. 65. Honoring exemplary teaching* (pp. 41–50). San Francisco: Jossey-Bass.

Fincher, C. (1994). Learning theory and research. In K. A. Feldman & M. B. Paulsen (Eds.), *Teaching and learning in the college classroom* (pp. 137–149). Needham Heights, MA: Ginn Press.

Friedlander, J., & MacDougall, P. (1992). Achieving student success through student involvement. *Community College Review, 20*(1), 20–28.

Gabelnick, F., MacGregor, J., Matthews, R., & Smith, B. (1990). Learning communities: Creating connections among students, faculty, and disciplines. In *New directions in teaching and learning: 41.* San Francisco: Jossey-Bass.

Gage, N. L. (1978). *The scientific basis of the art of teaching.* New York: Teachers College Press.

Gilbert, S. W. (1997). *Levers for change: TLTR workbook (Teaching, Learning & Technology Roundtable Program: Regional TLTR).* Washington, DC: American Association of Higher Education.

Gomez-Mejia, L. R., & Balkin. (1992). Determinants of faculty pay: An agency theory perspective. *Academy of Management Journal, 35*(5), 921–955.

Gonick, L., & Milliron, M. D. (2002, August/September). Creativity and convergence. *Converge.*

Griffith, M., & Connor, A. (1994). *Democracy's open door: The community college in America's future.* Portsmouth, NH: Boynton/Cook.

Guskin, A. E. (1994). Reducing student costs and enhancing student learning. *Change, 26*(4), 22–29.

Halttunen, L. G. (2002). Palomar College: A technological transformation. *Community College Journal, 73*(2), 26–31.

Hartle, T. W., & King, J. E. (1997). The end of equal opportunity in higher education? *The College Board Review, 181,* 8–15.

Healy, J. M. (1994). *Your child's growing mind: A practical guide to brain development and learning from birth to adolescence.* New York: Doubleday.

Higgins, C. S., Hawthorne, E. M., Cape, J. A., & Bell, L. (1994). The successful community college instructor: A profile for recruitment. *Community College Review, 21*(4), 27–36.

Hirsch, E. E. (1987). *Cultural literacy.* New York: Houghton Mifflin.

Hodgkinson, H. (1997, April). Diversity comes in all sizes and shapes. *School Business Affairs.*

Horn, L. J., Chen, X., & MPR Associates. (1998, May). *Toward resiliency: At-risk students who make it to college.* Washington, DC: U.S. Department of Education, Office of Educational Research and Improvement.

Hudgins, J. L., & Williams, S. K. (1997). Seizing the opportunity of institutional effectiveness. In J. E. Roueche, L. F. Johnson, S. D. Roueche, & Associates, *Embracing the tiger: The effectiveness debate and the community college* (pp. 53–67). Washington, DC: Community College Press.

Jackson, M. W. (1995). Skimming the surface or going deep? *PS: Political Science and Politics, 28*(3), 512–514.

Jenrette, M., & Hays, K. (1996). Honoring exemplary teaching: The two-year college setting. In M. Svinicki & R. J. Menges (Eds.), *New directions for teaching and learning: 65. Honoring exemplary teaching* (pp. 77–83). San Francisco: Jossey-Bass.

Johnson, S. L. (1997). Community college leadership in the age of technology. *Leadership Abstracts, 10*(5).

Johnstone, S. M., & Poulin, R. (2002). What does distance learning really cost? *Community College Journal, 73*(2), 14–20.

Katz, J., & Henry, M. (1988). *Turning professors into teachers.* New York: Macmillan.

Kelley, W., & Wilbur, L. (1970). *Teaching in the community-junior college.* New York: Appleton-Century-Crofts.

Kimball, B. A. (1988). Historia calamitatum. In B. A. Kimball (Ed.), *Teaching undergraduates* (pp. 11–22). Buffalo, NY: Prometheus Books.

King, T., & Bannon, E. (2002). *At what cost?* Washington, DC: The State PIRG's Higher Education Project.

Klemp, G. O., Jr. (1977). Three factors of success. In D. W. Vermilye (Ed.), *Relating work and education.* San Francisco: Jossey-Bass.

Knowles, M. S. (1973). *The adult learner: A neglected species.* Houston, TX: Gulf.

Knox, A. B. (1977). *Adult development and learning.* San Francisco: Jossey-Bass.

Koltai, L. (1993). Community colleges: Making winners out of ordinary people. In A. Levine (Ed.), *Higher learning in America 1980–2000* (pp. 100–113). Baltimore, MD: Johns Hopkins University Press.

Kotre, J. (1984). *Outliving the self: Generativity and the interpretation of lives.* Baltimore: Johns Hopkins University Press.

Kotter, J. P. (1995). Leading change: Why transformation efforts fail. *Harvard Business Review, 73*(2), 59–67.

Krathwohl, D., Bloom, B. S., & Masia, B. (Eds.). 1964). *Taxonomy of educational objectives: Handbook II. Affective domain.* New York: David McKay.

Kulik, J. A., Kulik, C. C., & Cohen. P. A. (1980). Effectiveness of computer-based college teaching: A meta-analysis of findings. *Review of Educational Research, 50,* 525–544.

Lawrence, J. H., & Blackburn, R. T. (1985). Faculty careers: Maturation, demographic, and historical effects. *Research in Higher Education, 22,* 135–154.

Leonard, G. B. (1969). *Education and ecstasy.* New York: Delacorte Press.

Lewis, K. G. (1986). Using an objective observation system to diagnose teaching problems. *The Journal of Staff, Program, & Organization Development, 4*(4), 81–90.

Lewis, K. G. (1997). Collecting information using class observation. In K. T. Brinko & R. J. Menges (Eds.), *Practically speaking: A sourcebook for instructional consultants in higher education* (pp. 29–52). Stillwater, OK: New Forums Press.

Light, R. J. (1990). Explorations with students and faculty about teaching, learning, and student life. *The Harvard Assessment Seminars.* Cambridge, MA: Harvard University Graduate School of Education and Kennedy School of Government.

Lowman, J. (1984). *Mastering the techniques of teaching.* San Francisco: Jossey-Bass.

Lowman, J. (1996). Characteristics of exemplary teachers. In M. D. Svinicki & R. J. Menges (Eds.), *New directions for teaching and learning: No. 65. Honoring exemplary teaching* (pp. 33–40). San Francisco: Jossey-Bass.

Mander, J. (1992). *In absence of the sacred: The failure of technology and the survival of the Indian nations.* San Francisco: Sierra Club Books.

Mann, C. C. (2002, September). Homeland insecurity. *The Atlantic Monthly,* pp. 82–102.

Mann, R. D., Arnold, S. M., Binder, J., Cytrunbaum, S., Ringwald, J., & Rosenwien, R. (1970). *The college classroom: Conflict, change, and learning.* New York: Wiley.

Marsh, H. W. (1987). Students' evaluations of university teaching: Research findings, methodological issues, and directions for future research. *International Journal of Educational Research, 11,* 253–388.

McCabe, R. H., & Day, P. R., Jr. (1998). *Developmental education: A twenty-first century social and economic imperative.* Mission Viejo, CA: League for Innovation in the Community College and The College Board.

McClenney, B. (1997). Productivity and effectiveness at the Community College of Denver. In J. E. Roueche, L. F. Johnson, S. D. Roueche, & Associates (Eds.), *Embracing the tiger: The effectiveness debate and the community college* (pp. 71–80). Washington, DC: Community College Press.

McKeachie, W. J. (1990). Research on college teaching: The historical background. *Journal of Educational Psychology, 82*(2), 189–200.

McKeachie, W. J. (1994). *Teaching tips: Strategies, research, and theory for college and university teachers.* Lexington, MA: Heath.

McWilliams, P. (1995). *The portable life 101.* Los Angeles, CA: Prelude Press.

Menges, R. J. (1991). The real world of teaching improvement: A faculty perspective. In M. Theall & J. Franklin (Eds.), *New directions for teaching and learning: 48. Effective practices for improving teaching* (pp. 21–38). San Francisco: Jossey-Bass.

Menges, R. J., Weimer, M., and Associates. (1996). *Teaching on solid ground: Using scholarship to improve practice.* San Francisco: Jossey-Bass.

Miles, M. B., & Huberman, A. M. (1994). *Qualitative data analysis: An expanded source-book* (2nd ed.). Thousand Oaks, CA: Sage.

Miller, R. I. (1972). *Evaluating faculty performance.* San Francisco: Jossey-Bass.

Milliron, M. D. (2001). Join the conversation on learning. *Michigan Community College Journal, 7*(1).

Milliron, M. D. (2002a, November/December). Getting a kick out of learning with technology. *Converge.*

Milliron, M. D. (2002b). A time for the community college: 21st century dynamics, trends, and imperatives. In N. Thomas, A. Lorenzo, & M. D. Milliron (Eds.), *A journey of discovery.* Phoenix: Innovation Press.

Milliron, M. D., & de los Santos, G. E. (2002). Making the most of community colleges. Commissioned by National Governors Association (NGA). White Paper, Winter Series.

Milliron, M. D., & Johnson, S. L. (2002, June/July). Avoiding the dialectic dialogue of dogmatic diatribes. *Converge.*

Milliron, M. D., & Leach, E. R. (1997). Community colleges winning through innovation: Taking on the changes and choices of leadership in the twenty-first century [Special edition]. *Leadership Abstracts.*

Milliron, M. D. & Miles, C. L. (1998). *Technology, learning, and community (TLC): Perspectives from teaching excellence award recipients.* Mission Viejo, CA: League for Innovation in the Community College and SCT.

Milliron, M. D. & Miles, C. L. (2000). *Taking a big picture look at technology, learning, and the community college.* Mission Viejo, CA: Innovation Press.

Milliron, M. D., & Miles, C. L. (2001, November/December). Education in a digital democracy: Leading the charge for learning about, with, and beyond technology. *Educause Review.*

Naisbitt, J. (1982). *Megatrends.* New York: Warner Books.

National Center for Education Statistics. (1996). *Remedial education at higher education institutions in Fall 1995* (NCES Publication No. 97-584). Washington, DC: U.S. Department of Education.

National Center for Education Statistics. (2002a). *The condition of education 2002.* Washington, DC: U.S. Government Printing Office.

National Center for Education Statistics. (2002b). *Digest of educational statistics, 2001.* Washington, DC: U.S. Government Printing Office.

National Commission on Excellence in Education. (1983). *A nation at risk: The imperative for educational reform.* Washington, DC: U.S. Department of Education.

O'Banion, T. (1989). The renaissance of innovation. In T. O'Banion (Ed.), *Innovation in the community college* (pp. 1–22). New York: ACE/Macmillan.

O'Banion, T. (1996). A learning college for the 21st century. *Community College Journal, 66*(3), 18–23.

O'Banion, T. (1997). *A learning college for the 21st century.* Phoenix: ACE/Oryx Press.

O'Banion, T. (1998, May). *The learning college of the twenty-first century.* Keynote address presented at the meeting of the National Institute for Staff and Organizational Development, Conference on Teaching and Leadership Excellence, Austin, TX.

O'Banion, T., & Milliron, M. D. (2001). College conversations on learning. *Learning Abstracts, 4*(5).

O'Neil, J. (1995). On schools as learning organizations: A conversation with Peter Senge. *Educational Leadership, 51*(7), 20–24.

Owens, J. S. (1991). Collaboration within the college. In D. Angel & M. DeVault (Eds.), *Conceptualizing 2000: Proactive planning.* Washington, DC: Community College Press.

Palmer, P. J. (1993). Good talk about good teaching: Improving teaching through conversation and community. *Change, 25*(6), 8–13.

Pascarella, E. T., & Terenzini, P. T. (1991). *How college affects students.* San Francisco: Jossey-Bass.

Paulsen, M. B., & Feldman, K. A. (1995). *Taking teaching seriously: Meeting the challenge of instructional improvement.* ASHE-ERIC Higher Education Report No. 2. Washington, DC: The George Washington University, Graduate School of Education and Human Development.

Pedersen, R. P. (2002). High-wire act. *Community College Week, 15*(6), 15, 18.

Peters, T. J., & Waterman, R. H. (1982). *In search of excellence.* New York: Warner Books.

Pittinsky, M. S. (2002). *The wired tower: Perspectives on the impact of the Internet on higher education.* Upper Saddle River, NJ: Financial Times/Prentice Hall.

Pullias, E. V. (1963). *Toward excellence in college teaching.* Dubuque, IA: Brown.

Richlin, L., & Manning, B. (1996). Using portfolios to document teaching excellence. In M. D. Svinicki & R. J. Menges (Eds.), *New directions for teaching and learning: No. 65. Honoring exemplary teaching* (pp. 65–70). San Francisco: Jossey-Bass.

Roueche, J. E. (1968). *Salvage, redirection, or custody? Remedial education in the community junior college.* Washington, DC: American Association of Community Colleges.

Roueche, J. E., & Baker, G. A. (1986). *Profiling excellence in America's schools.* Arlington, VA: American Association of School Administrators.

Roueche, J. E., & Baker, G. A. (1987). *Access and excellence: The open-door college.* Washington, DC: Community College Press.

Roueche, J. E., Baker, G. A. III, & Rose, R. R. (1989). *Shared vision: Transformational leadership in American community colleges.* Washington, DC: Community College Press.

Roueche, J. E., Ely, E. E., & Roueche, S. D. (2001). *In pursuit of excellence: The Community College of Denver.* Washington, DC: Community College Press.

Roueche, J. E., Johnson, L. F., & Roueche, S. D. (1997). *Embracing the tiger: The effectiveness debate and the community college.* Washington, DC: Community College Press.

Roueche, J. E., & Roueche, S. D. (1993). *Between a rock and a hard place: The at-risk student in the open-door college.* Washington, DC: Community College Press.

Roueche, J. E., & Roueche, S. D. (1999). *High stakes, high performance: Making remedial education work.* Washington, DC: Community College Press.

Roueche, J. E., & Roueche, S. D. (2001). From "wow" to "how": Possibilities to practice. *Community College Week Special Supplement on Technology Issue* (February 19), 11, 21.

Roueche, J. E., & Roueche, S. D. (2002): Online learning can be seductive. *Community College Week, Special Fall Supplement on Technology Issue, 3,* 9.

Roueche, J. E., Roueche, S. D., & Johnson, R. A. (2002). At our best: Facing the challenges. *Community College Journal, 72*(5), 10–14.

Roueche, J. E., Roueche, S. D., & Milliron, M. D. (1995). *Strangers in their own land: Part-time faculty in American community colleges,* Washington, DC: Community College Press.

Ruppert, S. S. (Ed.). 1994). *Charting higher education accountability: A sourcebook on state-level performance indicators.* Denver: Education Commission of the States.

Sax, L. J., Astin, S. L., Korn, W. S., & Mahoney, K. M. (2000). *The American freshman: National norms for fall 2000.* Los Angeles: Higher Education Research Institute.

Schoch, R. (1980). As Cal enters the 80s, there'll be some changes made. *California Monthly, 90*(3), 1–3.

Schön, D. A. (1987). *Educating the reflective practitioner: Toward a new design for teaching and learning in their professions.* San Francisco: Jossey-Bass.

Seldin, P. (1988). Evaluating college teaching. In R. E. Young & K. E. Eble (Eds.), *New directions for teaching and learning: No. 33. College teaching and learning: Preparing for new commitments* (pp. 47–56). San Francisco: Jossey-Bass.

Seymour, D. (1993). *On Q: Causing quality in higher education.* Phoenix: ACE/Oryx Press.

Shaw, R. G. (1989). Curriculum change in the community college: Pendulum swing or spiral soar? In T. O'Banion (Ed.), *Innovation in the community college* (pp. 23–45). New York: ACE/Macmillan.

Skinner, B. F. (1938). *The behavior of organisms: An experimental analysis.* New York: Appleton-Century-Crofts.

Skinner, B. F. (1953). *Science and human behavior.* New York: Macmillan.

Skinner, B. F. (1968). *The technology of teaching.* New York: Appleton-Century-Crofts.

Smith, P. (1990). *Killing the spirit: Higher education in America.* New York: Viking Press.

Smith, T. M., Young, B. A., Bae, Y., Chayand, S. P., & Alsalam, N. (1997). *The condition of education.* Washington, DC: U. S. Department of Education, Office of Educational Research and Improvement, National Center for Education Statistics.

Stanley, C. A. (2002). Factors that contribute to the teaching development of faculty development center clientele: A case study of ten university professors. In *Higher education as a field of inquiry: Informing the future* (pp. 83–103). College Station: Texas A&M University.

Starbuck, S. (2002, Spring). Place poems: Including a sense of place in the curriculum. In *Washington center news: Teaching and organizing for access and excellence* (pp. 20–22). Olympia, WA: Washington Center for Improving the Quality of Undergraduate Education.

Starhawk. (1979). *Spiral dance.* New York: Harper & Row.

Sternberg, R. J., & Horvath, J. A. (1995). A prototype view of expert teaching. *Educational Researcher, 24*(6), 9–17.

Sticht T., & McDonald, B. (1989, January). *Making the nation smarter: The intergenerational transfer of cognitive ability.* San Diego: Applied Behavioral and Cognitive Sciences, Inc. (ED No. 309 279).

Stokes, M. T., Halcomb, C. G., & Slovacek, C. P. (1988). Delaying user responses to computer-mediated test items enhances test performance. *Journal of Computer-Based Instruction, 15*(3), 99–103.

Svinicki, M. D. (1991). Practical implications of cognitive theories. In R. J. Menges & M. D. Svinicki (Eds.), *New directions for teaching and learning: 45. College teaching: From theory to practice* (pp. 27–37). San Francisco: Jossey-Bass.

Svinicki, M. D., Hagen, A. S., & Meyer, D. K. (1996). How research on learning strengthens instruction. In R. J. Menges, M. Weimer, & Associates (Eds.), *Teaching on solid ground: Using scholarship to improve practice* (pp. 257–288). San Francisco: Jossey-Bass.

Tang, T. L., & Chamberlain, M. (1997). Attitudes toward research and teaching. *Journal of Higher Education, 68*(2), 212–227.

Tarence, Z. (2002). A view from the outside in: Community colleges as entrepreneurial community learning centers. *Leadership Abstracts, 15*(11).

Thomas, G. W., & Ferguson, D. G. (1987). *In celebration of the teacher.* Las Cruces, NM: New Mexico State University Foundation.

Tinto, V. (1987). *Leaving college: Rethinking the causes and cures of student attrition.* Chicago: The University of Chicago Press.

Tudor, R. M., & Bostow, D. E. (1991). Computer programmed instruction: The relation of required interaction to practical application. *Journal of Applied Behavior Analysis, 24*(2), 361–368.

Ullom, J. (1989). Music series discs are popular in California. *Music Disc News, 1*(2), 8–9, 19.

Upcraft, M. L. (1996). Teaching and today's college students. In R. J. Menges, M. Weimer, & Associates (Eds.), *Teaching on solid ground* (pp. 21–41). San Francisco: Jossey-Bass.

Vaughan, G. B. (1994). The community college teacher as scholar. In T. O'Banion (Ed.), *Teaching and learning in the community college* (pp. 161–178). Washington, DC: Community College Press.

Walker, C. J., & Quinn, J. W. (1996). Fostering instructional vitality and motivation. In R. J. Menges, M. Weimer, & Associates, *Teaching on solid ground: Using scholarship to improve practice* (pp. 315–336). San Francisco: Jossey-Bass.

Ward, C. V. L. (2001). Measuring up 2000: A yardstick for community colleges? *Community College Journal, 72*(1), 36–39.

Weimer, M. (1996). Why scholarship is the bedrock of good teaching. In R. J. Menges, M. Weimer, & Associates (Eds.), *Teaching on solid ground* (pp. 1–12). San Francisco: Jossey-Bass.

Weinstein, C. E. (1992). Working hard is not the same thing as working smart. *Innovation Abstracts XIV* (5).

Weinstein, C. E. (2002). Learner control; The upside and the downside of online learning. *Innovation Abstracts XXIV* (25). Austin: The University of Texas.

Wellman, J. V. (2001, March/April). Assessing state accountability systems. *Change.*

Wheatley, M. J. (1994). *Leadership and the new science: Learning about organizations from an orderly universe.* San Francisco: Barrett-Koehler.

Wilson, C. D. (2002, March). The community college as a learning-centered organization. In N. Thomas, A. L. Lorenzo, & M. D. Milliron (Eds.), *Perspectives on the community college: A journey of discovery* (pp. 23–26). Phoenix: Innovations Press. Available from www.leaguestore.org.

Wilson, C. D., Miles, C. L., Baker, R. L., & Schoenberger, R. L. (2000). *Learning outcomes for the 21st century: Report of a community college study.* Mission Viejo, CA: League for Innovation in the Community College and The Pew Charitable Trusts.

Wilson, R. C., Gaff, J. G., Dienst, E. R., Wood, L., & Bavry, J. L. (1975). *College professors and their impact on students.* New York: Wiley.

Wotruba, T. R., & Wright, P. L. (1975). How to develop a teacher-rating instrument: A research approach. *Journal of Higher Education, 46*(6), 653–663.

Zwerling, L. S. (1976). *Second best: The crisis of the community college.* New York: McGraw-Hill.

Zwerling, L. S. (1988, January/February). The Miami-Dade story: Is it really number one? *Change,* pp. 10–23.

Appendix A

Five-Star Faculty Survey

NISOD Teaching Excellence Award Recipient,

The following survey is being conducted as part of an ongoing international study of teaching excellence award recipients in community and two-year colleges/institutes—The Five-Star Faculty Study. The following questionnaire begins the second phase of this study, during which over 6,000 teaching excellence award recipients will be surveyed. Please take the time to complete the following questionnaire and share your insights and opinions with your community college colleagues around the world. All individual survey information will be kept completely confidential and specific comments or opinions will only be attributed with permission of the submitter.

*The second half of this page lists the demographic information questions. **Page two** begins the series of questions related to faculty opinions and teaching strategies explored in phase one of the study.*

If you have additional comments, suggestions, or questions regarding this research project, please use the space provided on the last page of the survey or attach an additional sheet with your contribution.

***Thank you** for taking the time to complete this survey and this contribution to the teaching profession in the community college!*

Demographic Information

1. Respondent Code (see cover letter included with questionnaire) _____

2. Sex (circle one):   Male   Female

3. Age (in years) _____

4. Community college teaching experience (in years) _____

5. Total years teaching experience at all levels (in years) _____

6. Have you ever taught as a part-time faculty member at a community college (circle one)?
   Yes   No

7. The category that best describes the institution at which you teach (circle one)?
   a. Comprehensive Community College
   b. Technical College/Institute
   c. Junior College

8. Which category best describes the area in which your teaching discipline would fall (circle one)?
   a. General Education/Arts and Sciences
   b. Technical Education
   c. Vocational Education
   d. Continuing Education/Workforce Development

9. In what year were you honored as a *NISOD Teaching Excellence Award Recipient*? _____

10. How many (circle one) semester or quarter hours do you teach in a typical fall term? _____

11. Do you plan to retire in the next five years (circle one)? Yes No

Five-Star Faculty Teaching Questions

Instructions (read carefully):

The following charts contain the results of the first phase of the Five-Star Faculty Study. In phase one, over 200 Teaching Excellence Award Recipients helped explore key questions about teaching in the community college. These charts reflect a synthesis of over 3,000 comments from your fellow educators, all collected during five interactive focus groups conducted during the 1997 National Institute for Staff and Organizational Development (NISOD) *Teaching and Leadership Excellence Conference*. We ask that you review these data and supply reactions based on your experience and opinions.

For example, in response to question one, "What inspired you to become a teacher?", one cluster of responses from the focus groups related to the influence of **a positive role model**. This category title will be bulleted and followed by an actual comment from that cluster. The following scale will be listed to the left of the response category title:

YES! Yes yes ? no No NO!

Please circle the response that best reflects the intensity of your agreement/disagreement regarding this focus group response category. Circle the "?" response if you are neutral regarding the category, and leave the scale blank if you are unsure. In the column to the right, you should evaluate all the response categories to a given question and then **rank the top three (1, 2, 3)**, with one being the response category with which you most agree.

Therefore, if you strongly agree with the category of **a positive role model** in response to question one, and considered it the *number one reason* why you became a teacher, the row in the chart would look like this:

YES!	Yes	yes	?	no	No	NO!	**A positive role model**—"To do for others what teachers have done for me."	1

If you have any questions about how to fill in the following chart, please contact Sheryl Powell at the University of Texas at Austin, at (512) 471-7545.

1. What inspired you to become a teacher?

Your Reaction to FG Response							Your Reaction to FG Response	Top 3
YES!	Yes	yes	?	no	No	NO!	**A positive role model**—"To do for others what teachers have done for me."	
YES!	Yes	yes	?	no	No	NO!	**A negative role model**—"In law school, I had a very bad instructor. I vowed that if I ever taught, I would be completely unlike him."	
YES!	Yes	yes	?	no	No	NO!	**A desire to make a difference**—"The hope that I can make a difference in someone's life."	
YES!	Yes	yes	?	no	No	NO!	**The love of the subject**—"A desire to communicate my love of literature."	
YES!	Yes	yes	?	no	No	NO!	**The love of learning**—"To continue to be actively involved in learning."	
YES!	Yes	yes	?	no	No	NO!	**The love of people**—"Excitement of working with young people and returning adults."	
YES!	Yes	yes	?	no	No	NO!	**The love of teaching**—"Born with chalk dust in my blood."	
YES!	Yes	yes	?	no	No	NO!	**Family/friends/significant others**—"My father inspired me to become a teacher. Since I was a child, he always told me it was the most rewarding career of all!"	
YES!	Yes	yes	?	no	No	NO!	**Serendipity**—"Someone needed a teacher fast—and then I found my soul."	
YES!	Yes	yes	?	no	No	NO!	**Personal benefits**—"Job fit my personal needs."	

* **Survey Respondent Note:** The following two questions juxtapose the *teaching of content* and *the teaching of students*. We provide a brief explanation here to ensure that you receive the same description of the difference between teaching content and students that was offered to the focus group participants. The teaching of content question seeks information on the strategies used by teachers to relate specific subject matter to students. The teaching of students questions seek information on how teachers connect with the affective domain, with the students themselves. We are aware that separating these two foci is somewhat artificial; however, the distinction does provide some useful separation in strategies and has prompted some wonderfully thoughtful comments on the bridging of content and student foci in teaching.

2. What are the core strategies you use to be an effective teacher of content?

Your Reaction to FG Response	Your Reaction to FG Response	Top 3
YES! Yes yes ? no No NO!	**Strive to foster higher-level learning**—"Simulations that require analysis, problem solving, and critical thinking."	
YES! Yes yes ? no No NO!	**Set high expectations/give challenging work**—"Have high expectations of your students, hold them to standards, and don't get in the habit of 'letting things slide'."	
YES! Yes yes ? no No NO!	**Use a variety of methods**—"Making sure I use or address three learning modalities—audio, visual, kinesthetic—in each lesson I teach."	
YES! Yes yes ? no No NO!	**Be organized**—"Organize information carefully so that it's easier for students to learn."	
YES! Yes yes ? no No NO!	**Emphasize relevance, application, and utility**—"Reinforce theory constantly with real-world applications."	
YES! Yes yes ? no No NO!	**Know your subject**—"Keeping my intellect stimulated: reading, writing, and changing the content of my syllabus so I stay fresh."	
YES! Yes yes ? no No NO!	**Utilize group work/collaborative learning**—"Use small group activities to encourage/enable high level of discussion."	
YES! Yes yes ? no No NO!	**Conduct classroom research**—"Have students share muddy thoughts at close of class."	
YES! Yes yes ? no No NO!	**Actively involve students**—"If students are to learn, they must speak!"	

2. What are the core strategies you use to be an effective teacher of content? (cont'd)

Your Reaction to FG Response							Your Reaction to FG Response	Top 3
YES!	Yes	yes	?	no	No	NO!	**Be student centered**—"My lesson plans content is adjusted to meet individual needs of student."	
YES!	Yes	yes	?	no	No	NO!	**Provide learning resources**—"Pre-typed outlines are given to students so they do not have to spend all their effort in writing down information frantically."	
YES!	Yes	yes	?	no	No	NO!	**Make use of visuals**—"I try to create visuals to explain concepts."	
YES!	Yes	yes	?	no	No	NO!	**Use humor**—"Humor, yes, it makes a big difference, but you must know how to use it effectively."	
YES!	Yes	yes	?	no	No	NO!	**Communicate clearly**—"Use vocabulary that students are already familiar with until they 'get' the concept."	
YES!	Yes	yes	?	no	No	NO!	**Test/assess well**—"Demonstration of understanding vis-à-vis exams, discussions, debates, presentations, simulations, and debriefings."	
YES!	Yes	yes	?	no	No	NO!	**Use technology to its fullest**—"Use technological resources available."	
YES!	Yes	yes	?	no	No	NO!	**Affirm and redirect as necessary**—"No matter what answer is offered in discussion, I affirm it in some way, and then move on and reinforce the correct answer."	

3. What strategies do you use to be an effective teacher of students?

Your Reaction to FG Response							Your Reaction to FG Response	Top 3
YES!	Yes	yes	?	no	No	NO!	**Make contact**—"Find out about each student. Remember names!"	
YES!	Yes	yes	?	no	No	NO!	**Show respect**—"Always treat students as important human beings."	
YES!	Yes	yes	?	no	No	NO!	**Demonstrate care and empathy**—"Each student is important—your caring is often the turning point in their education/life."	
YES!	Yes	yes	?	no	No	NO!	**Hold to high expectations**—"Raise the levels of expectations and don't pander to mediocrity! If you expect more, you get more."	

3. What strategies do you use to be an effective teacher of students? (cont'd)

Your Reaction to FG Response	Your Reaction to FG Response	Top 3
YES! Yes yes ? no No NO!	**Encourage humor and humanity**—"Maintaining a sense of humor—especially about myself and my subject."	
YES! Yes yes ? no No NO!	**Be enthusiastic/share joy**—"I share my joy at being with them and my excitement about the importance of our topic—it works well."	
YES! Yes yes ? no No NO!	**Foster student motivation/success skills**—"Help students develop the tools and confidence to take responsibility for their own learning."	
YES! Yes yes ? no No NO!	**Praise/celebrate/reward students**—"Praise them, encourage them, keep a sheet handy of 100 encouraging phrases."	
YES! Yes yes ? no No NO!	**Walk your talk**—"Role model—in all you do demonstrate good communication skills, study skills, time management skills."	
YES! Yes yes ? no No NO!	**Be flexible**—"Be flexible and willing to try another approach when your favorite one is not working."	
YES! Yes yes ? no No NO!	**Listen to students** —"Above all, be a good listener."	

4. How do you know learning is going on?

Your Reaction to FG Response	Your Reaction to FG Response	Top 3
YES! Yes yes ? no No NO!	**Formal testing**—"Testing: Ask essay questions that require application of content. Multiple choice can also require critical thinking."	
YES! Yes yes ? no No NO!	**Verbal feedback**—"Ask student(s) to paraphrase major ideas."	
YES! Yes yes ? no No NO!	**Nonverbal feedback**—"Informally, by the look in the eyes—the engaged expression."	
YES! Yes yes ? no No NO!	**Written feedback**—"I ask students to write what they have learned in a particular session. The papers are usually 50 words or less."	
YES! Yes yes ? no No NO!	**Third-person reports**—"Employers call me to get students to apply at their law firms because they have other successful students of mine as employees."	

4. How do you know learning is going on? (cont'd)

Your Reaction to FG Response							Your Reaction to FG Response	Top 3
YES!	Yes	yes	?	no	No	NO!	**Applications**—"Direct observation of student performance and application of theory in a 'live' setting."	
YES!	Yes	yes	?	no	No	NO!	**Group work**—"Listen in during group work."	
YES!	Yes	yes	?	no	No	NO!	**Outside-of-class interactions**—"When we discuss issue/topics/concerns that were addressed in the classroom, outside the classroom."	
YES!	Yes	yes	?	no	No	NO!	**Helping/teaching others**—"When a student can explain a concept to another student, especially when it involves an extension of a concept to a new application."	
YES!	Yes	yes	?	no	No	NO!	**We don't**—"Difficult to know, especially in the humanities and history."	

5. In what ways do you use information technology in instruction?

Your Reaction to FG Response							Your Reaction to FG Response	Top 3
YES!	Yes	yes	?	no	No	NO!	**Technology for communication/interactions**—"My students can reach me 24 hours a day for chats via e-mail or fax."	
YES!	Yes	yes	?	no	No	NO!	**Technology for presentation**—"Use PowerPoint to create classroom presentations and student handouts—it's been a God-send."	
YES!	Yes	yes	?	no	No	NO!	**Technology for research and reference**—"I assign Internet research."	
YES!	Yes	yes	?	no	No	NO!	**Technology for assessment**—"Use QuestionMark software to design and deliver testing online."	
YES!	Yes	yes	?	no	No	NO!	**Technology for course management**—"I put my syllabus online, collect papers via e-mail, and produce grade sheets on spreadsheets."	
YES!	Yes	yes	?	no	No	NO!	**Technology for student application/production**—"I expect all work to look professional and have students use word processor, spreadsheets, and PowerPoint to prepare their assignments to make sure it does."	

5. In what ways do you use information technology in instruction? (cont'd)

Your Reaction to FG Response							Your Reaction to FG Response	Top 3
YES!	Yes	yes	?	no	No	NO!	**Technology for student-driven learning**—"There are some self-paced computer programs on some of our syllabi content—students can do these programs in the computer lab and come to class prepared to move beyond the program in a higher level of discussion on that topic."	

6. What do you see as the key issues (positives or problems) in the use of technology in instruction?

Your Reaction to FG Response							Your Reaction to FG Response	Top 3
YES!	Yes	yes	?	no	No	NO!	**It takes a lot of time and training to use well**—"Changes so fast that staying current is difficult."	
YES!	Yes	yes	?	no	No	NO!	**There's a great deal of fear/resistance around the use of technology**—"Resistance to learning new techniques—both students and faculty—but more faculty."	
YES!	Yes	yes	?	no	No	NO!	**It's becoming a "basic skill" our students need**—"Students will be exposed to high tech on their first job. They must use current technology to succeed."	
YES!	Yes	yes	?	no	No	NO!	**The hardware and software can be problematic**—"Hardware/software problems are very time consuming and distracting."	
YES!	Yes	yes	?	no	No	NO!	**Some are tempted to use technology for the novelty, not the utility**—"More focus on gadgets than on students and learning."	
YES!	Yes	yes	?	no	No	NO!	**It can make your teaching more engaging**—"The ability to make the classroom or the course work experience more exciting."	
YES!	Yes	yes	?	no	No	NO!	**It can get very expensive**—"Computer labs are expensive to set up and become outdated the day of the grand opening (also expensive to maintain)."	
YES!	Yes	yes	?	no	No	NO!	**Students don't have equal access to technology**—"Not all students have access to computers/Internet either on or off campus."	

6. What do you see as the key issues (positives or problems) in the use of technology in instruction? (cont'd)

Your Reaction to FG Response							Your Reaction to FG Response	Top 3
YES!	Yes	yes	?	no	No	NO!	**Can help facilitate different kinds of learning—** "Giving students more avenues of learning—some are readers, some are watchers, and some are listeners."	
YES!	Yes	yes	?	no	No	NO!	**Gives students more control of learning (e.g., asynchronous learning)—**"Students can work in self-directed fashion—it bridges time and space gaps."	
YES!	Yes	yes	?	no	No	NO!	**True believers can cause problems—**"Techno-able folks patronizing the techno-novice. No one wants to learn something they have been made to feel inadequate about."	
YES!	Yes	yes	?	no	No	NO!	**Need to keep the human touch—**"With Internet courses and interactive TV, students can some-times feel alienated."	

7. What advice would you give a beginning community college instructor?

Your Reaction to FG Response							Your Reaction to FG Response	Top 3
YES!	Yes	yes	?	no	No	NO!	**Find a mentor—**"Get a mentor—select one who will actively help you understand how to grow as a teacher, and to thrive in the department and col-lege; one who will encourage you and challenge you to do your best."	
YES!	Yes	yes	?	no	No	NO!	**Focus on your students—**"Your primary commit-ment is to students—keep your focus on that despite the fact that other things could consume your attention."	
YES!	Yes	yes	?	no	No	NO!	**Orient yourself to the community college context and your college in particular—**"Be aware of the community college student demographics early on."	
YES!	Yes	yes	?	no	No	NO!	**Put forth the effort necessary to be effective—** "Work hard, come to class on time, come pre-pared, and stay the whole time."	

7. What advice would you give a beginning community college instructor? (cont'd)

Your Reaction to FG Response							Your Reaction to FG Response	Top 3
YES!	Yes	yes	?	no	No	NO!	**Be positive**—"Always be positive—use positive comments and encouragement as much as possible."	
YES!	Yes	yes	?	no	No	NO!	**Strive for balance**—"Keep up your development, both content and personal."	
YES!	Yes	yes	?	no	No	NO!	**Set high standards for self and students**—"Hold your students to high standards, but build in small successes along the way to encourage them as they struggle to meet the high standard."	
YES!	Yes	yes	?	no	No	NO!	**Explore and utilize a range of teaching techniques**—"Take a course in teaching strategies if you have had no formal teaching/education background—don't be afraid to try something new!"	
YES!	Yes	yes	?	no	No	NO!	**Value student contributions**—"Never underestimate what students bring with them to the classroom."	
YES!	Yes	yes	?	no	No	NO!	**Get involved in college activities**—"Attend as many school functions as possible."	
YES!	Yes	yes	?	no	No	NO!	**Be flexible**—"Be very flexible—a must."	
YES!	Yes	yes	?	no	No	NO!	**Be open and honest**—"Tell the truth. There is nothing so deadly as trying to fake it in front of students, especially if there are working adults in the class."	
YES!	Yes	yes	?	no	No	NO!	**Embrace teaching life**—"You don't just teach curriculum—you teach life."	
YES!	Yes	yes	?	no	No	NO!	**Value the intrinsic rewards**—"Don't expect to get RICH in material terms, but DO expect a GREAT and exciting life."	

Closing Comments: Phase three of this study will involve conducting focus groups with community college students (current and former) to explore their reactions/responses to the data from phase one and two. If you have any comments, questions, or suggestions for the research team as they proceed, please record them below or on an attached sheet.

Comments, suggestions, or concerns:

Thank you for taking the time to complete this survey!

Please use the self-addressed stamped envelope enclosed in the survey packet to mail the completed form to:

Sheryl Powell
The University of Texas at Austin
Community College Leadership Program
SZB 348
Austin, TX 78712
Tel: (512) 471-7545; Fax: (512) 471-9426

Appendix B

Results of the Five-Star Faculty Survey
Preliminary Data Based on *n* = 1,670 Respondents

Demographic Information

1. Name

2. Sex
   44.3% Male   **55.7%** Female

3. Age (in years)
   Mean = 50.27; mode = 50.0
   Range = 27–85

4. Community college teaching experience (in years)
   Mean = 17.43

5. Total FT teaching experience at all levels (in years)
   Full-time: Mean = 19.54
   Part-time: Mean = 4.84

6. Race/Ethnicity?
   91.4% White   **3.0%** Hispanic   **2.8%** African American/Black   **1.6%** Other

7. The category that best describes the institution at which you teach?
   89.6% Community College District
   4.7% Non-district affiliated > 8,000
   5.7% Non-district affiliated > 8,000

8. Which category best describes the area in which your teaching discipline would fall?
   67.1% General Education/Arts and Sciences
   30.7% Technical Education
   2.2% Continuing Education/Workforce Development

9. In what year were you honored as a *NISOD Teaching Excellence Award Recipient*?

1989	1991	1992	1993	1994	1995	1996	1997
2.4%	4.0%	9.7%	13.9%	15.5%	19.8%	16.6%	18.1%

10. Number of semester or quarter hours you teach in a typical fall term?
    Invalid Question—Responses ignored

11. Do you plan to retire in the next five years? **24%** Yes   **76%** No

1. What inspired you to become a teacher?

YES! 1	Yes 2	yes 3	Neutral 4	no 5	No 6	NO! 7	Mean Score	Focus Group (FG) Responses to the Above Question	Rank
53%	29%	14%	3%	1%	0%	0%	1.7	**A desire to make a difference**—"The hope that I can make a difference in someone's life."	1
41%	32%	16%	7%	2%	1%	1%	2.0	**The love of the subject**—"A desire to communicate my love of literature."	2
45%	35%	15%	4%	1%	1%	0%	1.8	**The love of learning**—"To continue to be actively involved in learning."	3
38%	34%	20%	6%	1%	1%	0%	2.0	**The love of people**—"Excitement of working with young people and returning adults."	4
28%	29%	23%	13%	5%	3%	1%	2.5	**A positive role model**—"To do for others what teachers have done for me."	5
30%	27%	19%	13%	6%	3%	3%	2.6	**The love of teaching**—"Born with chalk dust in my blood."	6
12%	20%	29%	16%	7%	8%	8%	3.4	**Personal benefits**—"Job fit my personal needs."	7
10%	9%	12%	19%	14%	13%	24%	4.5	**Serendipity**—"Someone needed a teacher fast— and then I found my soul."	8
7%	11%	15%	26%	17%	13%	12%	4.2	**Family/friends/significant others**—"My father inspired me to become a teacher. Since I was a child, he always told me it was the most rewarding career of all!"	9
7%	8%	14%	17%	12%	18%	24%	4.7	**A negative role model**—"In law school, I had a very bad instructor. I vowed that if I ever taught, I would be completely unlike him."	10

2. What are the core strategies you use to be an effective teacher of content?

YES! 1	Yes 2	yes 3	Neutral 4	no 5	No 6	NO! 7	Mean Score	Focus Group (FG) Responses to the Above Question	Rank
57%	31%	10%	2%	0%	0%	0%	1.6	**Know your subject**—"Keeping my intellect stimulated: reading, writing, and changing the content of my syllabus so I stay fresh."	1
57%	29%	12%	2%	0%	0%	0%	1.6	**Emphasize relevance, application, and utility**— "Reinforce theory constantly with "real-world" applications."	2
51%	32%	13%	2%	1%	0%	0%	1.7	**Be Organized**—"Organize information carefully so that it's easier for students to learn."	3
41%	40%	15%	3%	1%	0%	0%	1.8	**Set high expectations/give challenging work**— "Have high expectations of your students, hold them to standards, and don't get in the habit of 'letting things slide'."	4
39%	39%	18%	3%	1%	0%	0%	1.9	**Strive to foster higher-level learning**—"Simulations that require analysis, problem solving, and critical thinking."	5

2. What are the core strategies you use to be an effective teacher of content? (cont'd)

YES! 1	Yes 2	yes 3	Neutral 4	no 5	No 6	NO! 7	Mean Score	Focus Group (FG) Responses to the Above Question	Rank
41%	30%	22%	5%	1%	0%	0%	2.0	**Actively involve students**—"If students are to learn, they must speak!"	6
35%	31%	20%	8%	5%	1%	0%	2.2	**Use a variety of methods**—"Making sure I use or address three learning modalities—audio, visual, kinesthetic—in each lesson I teach."	7
30%	29%	25%	9%	5%	1%	1%	2.4	**Be student centered**—"My lesson plan's content is adjusted to meet individual needs of student."	8
40%	34%	20%	5%	1%	0%	0%	2.0	**Use humor**—"Humor, yes, it makes a big difference, but you must know how to use it effectively."	9
39%	40%	17%	4%	1%	0%	0%	1.9	**Communicate clearly**—"Use vocabulary that students are already familiar with until they 'get' the concept."	10
22%	30%	28%	10%	6%	3%	2%	2.6	**Utilize group work/collaborative learning**—"Use small group activities to encourage/enable high level of discussion."	11
27%	39%	24%	7%	2%	1%	0%	2.2	**Affirm and redirect as necessary**—"No matter what answer is offered in discussion, I affirm it in some way, and then reinforce the correct answer."	12
22%	28%	27%	13%	7%	3%	1%	2.7	**Use technology to its fullest**—"Use technological resources available."	13
31%	33%	26%	6%	3%	1%	0%	2.2	**Make use of visuals**—"I try to create visuals to explain concepts."	14
21%	24%	23%	12%	12%	6%	3%	3.0	**Provide learning resources**—"Pre-typed outlines are given to students so they do not have to spend all their effort in writing down information frantically."	15
24%	43%	25%	6%	1%	0%	0%	2.2	**Test/assess well**—"Demonstration of understanding vis-à-vis exams, discussions, debates, presentations, simulations, and debriefings."	16
5%	16%	27%	26%	18%	6%	2%	3.6	**Conduct classroom research**—"Have students share muddy thoughts at close of class."	17

3. What strategies do you use to be an effective teacher of students?

YES! 1	Yes 2	yes 3	Neutral 4	no 5	No 6	NO! 7	Mean Score	Focus Group (FG) Responses to the Above Question	Rank
73%	21%	5%	1%	0%	0%	0%	1.3	**Show respect**—"Always treat students as important human beings."	1
62%	28%	9%	1%	0%	0%	0%	1.5	**Be enthusiastic/share joy**—"I share my joy at being with them and my excitement about the importance of our topic—it works well."	2
58%	31%	10%	2%	0%	0%	0%	1.6	**Demonstrate care and empathy**—"Each student is important—your caring is often the turning point in their education/life."	3
48%	37%	12%	3%	1%	0%	0%	1.7	**Hold to high expectations**—"Raise the levels of expectations and don't pander to mediocrity! If you expect more, you get more."	4
50%	35%	13%	2%	0%	0%	0%	1.7	**Walk your talk**—"Role model—in all you do demonstrate good communication skills, study skills, time management skills."	5
45%	38%	15%	2%	0%	0%	0%	1.7	**Foster student motivation/success skills**—"Help students develop the tools and confidence to take responsibility for their own learning."	6
43%	30%	21%	3%	2%	0%	0%	1.9	**Make contact**—"Find out about each student. Remember names!"	7
53%	33%	13%	1%	0%	0%	0%	1.6	**Listen to students** —"Above all, be a good listener."	8
47%	39%	12%	2%	0%	0%	0%	1.7	**Encourage humor and humanity**—"Maintaining a sense of humor—especially about myself and my subject."	9
43%	41%	14%	2%	0%	0%	0%	1.8	**Be flexible**—"Be flexible and willing to try another approach when your favorite one is not working."	10
29%	35%	23%	9%	3%	1%	0%	2.3	**Praise/celebrate/reward students**—"Praise them, encourage them, keep a sheet handy of 100 encouraging phrases."	11

4. How do you know learning is going on?

YES! 1	Yes 2	yes 3	Neutral 4	no 5	No 6	NO! 7	Mean Score	Focus Group (FG) Responses to the Above Question	Rank
43%	33%	15%	6%	2%	1%	1%	2.0	**Formal testing**—"Testing—ask essay questions that require application of content. Multiple choice can also require critical thinking."	1
34%	22%	18%	15%	7%	3%	2%	2.5	**Applications**—"Direct observation of student performance and application of theory in a 'live' setting."	2
27%	39%	25%	6%	3%	0%	1%	2.2	**Verbal feedback**—"Ask student(s) to paraphrase major ideas."	3

4. How do you know learning is going on? (cont'd)

YES! 1	Yes 2	yes 3	Neutral 4	no 5	No 6	NO! 7	Mean Score	Focus Group (FG) Responses to the Above Question	Rank
27%	34%	27%	8%	2%	1%	1%	2.3	**Nonverbal feedback**—"Informally, by the look in the eyes—the engaged expression."	4
32%	33%	27%	6%	2%	1%	0%	2.2	**Helping/teaching others**—"When a student can explain a concept to another student, especially when it involves an extension of a concept to a new application."	5
15%	20%	21%	18%	18%	6%	3%	3.3	**Written feedback**—"I ask students to write what they have learned in a particular session. The papers are usually 50 words or less."	6
20%	29%	29%	13%	6%	2%	2%	2.7	**Group work**—"Listen in during group work."	7
14%	25%	33%	18%	7%	2%	1%	2.9	**Outside-of-class interactions**—"When we discuss issue/topics/concerns that were addressed in the classroom, outside the classroom."	8
12%	18%	22%	25%	12%	6%	5%	3.5	**Third-person reports**—"Employers call me to get students to apply at their law firms because they have other successful students of mine as employees."	9
2%	4%	6%	41%	10%	13%	25%	5.0	**We don't**—"Difficult to know, especially in the humanities and history."	10

5. In what ways do you use information technology in instruction?

YES! 1	Yes 2	yes 3	Neutral 4	no 5	No 6	NO! 7	Mean Score	Focus Group (FG) Responses to the Above Question	Rank
19%	19%	21%	14%	15%	6%	6%	3.3	**Technology for student application/production**—"I expect all work to look professional and have students use word processor, spreadsheets, and PowerPoint to prepare their assignments to make sure it does."	1
18%	18%	21%	15%	15%	6%	7%	3.4	**Technology for student-driven learning** —"There are some self-paced computer programs on some of our syllabi content—students can do these programs in the computer lab and come to class prepared to move beyond the program in a higher level of discussion on that topic."	2
17%	13%	18%	15%	18%	9%	10%	3.7	**Technology for presentation**—"Use PowerPoint to create classroom presentations and student handouts—it's been a God-send."	3
20%	13%	17%	11%	16%	9%	14%	3.7	**Technology for communication/interactions**—"My students can reach me 24 hours a day for chats via e-mail or fax."	4
13%	16%	24%	14%	17%	8%	8%	3.6	**Technology for research and reference**—"I assign Internet research."	5

5. In what ways do you use information technology in instruction? (cont'd)

YES! 1	Yes 2	yes 3	Neutral 4	no 5	No 6	NO! 7	Mean Score	Focus Group (FG) Responses to the Above Question	Rank
8%	9%	14%	13%	29%	12%	16%	4.5	**Technology for course management**—"I put my syllabus online, collect papers via e-mail, and produce grade sheets on spreadsheets."	6
3%	4%	7%	18%	33%	16%	20%	5.0	**Technology for assessment**—"Use QuestionMark software to design and deliver testing online."	7

Note: *Question 5.8 (Family, Friends, and Significant Others) was mistakenly duplicated here from Question 1.8. Although ignored in the summary above, it was rated the 7th most important factor.*

6. What do you see as the key issues (positives or problems) in the use of technology in instruction?

YES! 1	Yes 2	yes 3	Neutral 4	no 5	No 6	NO! 7	Mean Score	Focus Group (FG) Responses to the Above Question	Rank
50%	29%	16%	4%	1%	0%	0%	1.8	**It's becoming a "basic skill" our students need**—"Students will be exposed to high tech on their first job. They must use current technology to succeed."	1
35%	30%	23%	5%	4%	2%	1%	2.2	**It takes a lot of time and training to use well**—"Changes so fast that staying current is difficult."	2
33%	23%	25%	13%	4%	2%	1%	2.4	**Need to keep the human touch**—"With Internet courses and interactive TV, students can sometimes feel alienated."	3
26%	33%	25%	12%	3%	1%	0%	2.4	**It can make your teaching more engaging**—"The ability to make the classroom or the course work experience more exciting."	4
31%	37%	24%	6%	1%	0%	0%	2.1	**Can help facilitate different kinds of learning**—"Giving students more avenues of learning—some are readers, some are watchers, and some are listeners."	5
37%	27%	22%	10%	3%	1%	1%	2.2	**It can get very expensive**—"Computer labs are expensive to set up and become outdated the day of the grand opening (also expensive to maintain)."	6
30%	24%	22%	9%	8%	4%	4%	2.7	**Students don't have equal access to technology**—"Not all students have access to computers/Internet either on or off campus."	7
21%	25%	30%	14%	7%	2%	1%	2.7	**The hardware and software can be problematic**—"Hardware/software problems are very time consuming and distracting."	8
22%	33%	26%	15%	3%	1%	0%	2.5	**Gives students more control of learning (e.g., asynchronous learning)**—"Students can work in self-directed fashion—it bridges time and space gaps."	9
16%	22%	28%	19%	10%	4%	2%	3.1	**Some are tempted to use technology for the novelty, not the utility**—"More focus on gadgets than on students and learning."	10

6. What do you see as the key issues (positives or problems) in the use of technology in instruction? (cont'd)

YES! 1	Yes 2	yes 3	Neutral 4	no 5	No 6	NO! 7	Mean Score	Focus Group (FG) Responses to the Above Question	Rank
15%	25%	29%	14%	11%	4%	3%	3.0	**There's a great deal of fear/resistance around the use of technology**—"Resistance to learning new techniques—students and faculty—but more faculty."	11
10%	17%	27%	28%	11%	4%	2%	3.4	**True believers can cause problems**—"Techno-able folks patronizing the techno-novice. No one wants to learn something they've been made to feel inadequate about."	12

7. What advice would you give a beginning community college instructor?

YES! 1	Yes 2	yes 3	Neutral 4	no 5	No 6	NO! 7	Mean Score	Focus Group (FG) Responses to the Above Question	Rank
68%	23%	7%	1%	0%	0%	0%	1.4	**Focus on your students**—"Your primary commitment is to students—keep your focus on that despite the fact that other things could consume your attention."	1
76%	18%	5%	0%	0%	0%	0%	1.3	**Put forth the effort necessary to be effective**—"Work hard, come to class on time, come prepared, and stay the whole time."	2
49%	26%	17%	7%	1%	0%	1%	1.9	**Find a mentor**—"Get a mentor—select one who will actively help you understand how to grow as a teacher, and to thrive in the department and college; one who will encourage you and challenge you to do your best."	3
68%	23%	7%	1%	0%	0%	0%	1.4	**Be positive**—"Always be positive—use positive comments and encouragement as much as possible."	4
59%	32%	9%	1%	0%	0%	0%	1.5	**Set high standards for self and students**—"Hold your students to high standards but build in small successes along the way to encourage them as they struggle to meet the high standard."	5
66%	26%	7%	1%	0%	0%	0%	1.5	**Be open and honest**—"Tell the truth. There is nothing so deadly as trying to fake it in front of students, especially if there are working adults in the class."	6
53%	31%	13%	3%	1%	0%	0%	1.7	**Explore and utilize a range of teaching techniques**—"Take a course in teaching strategies if you have had no formal teaching/education background—don't be afraid to try something new!"	7
49%	30%	14%	6%	1%	0%	0%	1.8	**Embrace teaching life**—"You don't just teach curriculum—you teach life."	8
42%	38%	18%	2%	0%	0%	0%	1.8	**Strive for balance**—"Keep up your development, both content and personal."	9

7. What advice would you give a beginning community college instructor? (cont'd)

YES! 1	Yes 2	yes 3	Neutral 4	no 5	No 6	NO! 7	Mean Score	Focus Group (FG) Responses to the Above Question	Rank
53%	32%	14%	1%	0%	0%	0%	1.7	**Value student contributions**—"Never underestimate what students bring with them to the classroom."	10
43%	34%	19%	4%	0%	0%	0%	1.9	**Be flexible**—"Be very flexible—a must."	11
48%	32%	14%	5%	0%	0%	0%	1.8	**Value the intrinsic rewards**—"Don't expect to get RICH in material terms, but DO expect a GREAT and exciting life."	12
31%	38%	24%	5%	1%	0%	0%	2.1	**Orient yourself to the community college context and your college in particular**—"Be aware of community college student demographics early on."	13
17%	26%	31%	19%	4%	2%	1%	2.8	**Get involved in college activities**—"Attend as many school functions as possible."	14

About the Authors

John E. Roueche is Sid W. Richardson Regents Chair and director of the Community College Leadership Program at The University of Texas at Austin. Author of 34 books and more than 150 articles and monographs on educational leadership and teaching effectiveness, Roueche has spoken to more than 1,300 colleges and universities since 1970. He received the 1986 National Leadership Award from the American Association of Community Colleges and the 1999 Career Research Excellence Award from The University of Texas at Austin.

Mark D. Milliron is the president and CEO of the League for Innovation in the Community College (www.league.org), an international consortium that has been catalyzing the community college movement for more than 35 years. Milliron is a Distinguished Graduate of The University of Texas at Austin, where he received his PhD. He has won numerous awards for his work exploring teaching excellence, student success strategies, leadership development, future trends, and the human side of technology change. He writes books, monographs, and articles; speaks at colleges, corporations, and conferences across the country and around the world; teaches in executive leadership and graduate programs; participates as a key resource for local, state, and national government programs; and serves as a member of several higher education and corporate boards.

Suanne D. Roueche is a senior lecturer in the Department of Educational Administration at The University of Texas at Austin. She directed the National Institute for Staff and Organizational Development (NISOD) for 20 years and now serves as editor of NISOD publications. Author of 14 books and more than 50 articles and book chapters, Roueche received the 1997 National Leadership Award from the American Association of Community Colleges.

Index

academic performance, challenges to successful, 7

active inquiry about teaching and learning, 48

Adelman, C., 152

adult learning theory, 45–46

affect, 81

affinity diagramming, 19

affirmation, 74

American Association of Colleges and Universities (AACU), 5

andragogy, 45

Angelo, T. A., 50–54, 100

assessing learning, 75–76. *See also* teaching, methods of evaluating
    methods of, 104, 108–110
        applications, 105
        formal testing, 104
        helping/teaching others and group work, 106–107
        limitations in, 108
        nonverbal feedback, 106
        outside-of-class interactions and third-person reports, 107–108
        verbal and written feedback, 105–106
    purposefully, systematically, and in timely manner, 155–156

Astin, A. W., 8

attribute-treatment interactions, 47

Baker, G. A., 55–57

Barnes, C. P., 48

Barr, R. B., 46

Bergquist, W. H., 99

Boyer, E. L., 49

Brookfield, S. D., 44

budgets, tighter, 9

"caring climate," creating a, 84

Carlzon, Jan, 157

celebration of the power of making a difference, 149–151

celebration, 92–93

Chickering, A. W., 55–57

classroom research, conducting, 76–77

cognitive factors in learning, 51–52
    surface processing and deep processing, 41

cognitive learning theory, 44–45

collaborative learning, 42, 73–74

college activities, involvement in, 145

communication, 117. *See also* listening
    clear, 72–73

community college mission statements, 8

Community College of Denver (CCD), 99–100

community colleges. *See also specific topics*
    centrality of learning and institutional effectiveness, 97–98
    competition among, 11–12
    increasing demands for institutional accountability, 8–9
    self-definition, 103

competition among education providers, increasing, 11–12

computer-enabled learning, 43

concern, demonstrating, 84–86

Coné, J., 10

cooperative learning. *See* collaborative learning

Cross, K. P., 41

demographics, student continuing shifts in, 6–7

discussion, 41

e-learning. *See* information technology (IT) applications; technology

Eble, K. E., 40, 151–153, 157

education. *See also specific topics*
    shifts in purposes of, 4–6
    typologies of best practices in undergraduate, 44
        conceptual progress, 44–47

methodological progress, 47–48
of the whole person, 151–152
education milieu, challenges posed
　　by, 4–13
Ellner, C. L., 48
emotion, 81
empathy, demonstrating, 84–86
"employee of the month," 150
employers, and purposes of education, 5
excitement, creating intellectual, 54, 102
expectations, holding to high, 67–68,
　　86–87, 138–139

faculty, college
　　and purposes of education, 6
feedback. *See under* assessing learning
"feeling" dimension of teaching, 81
Feldman, K. A., 55–57
Five-Star Faculty Survey, 20–21, 165–175
　　results of, 22, 176–184
flexibility, 92, 143
focus group, interactive qualitative, 19–20
funding, declining, 9

Gamson, Z. E., 55–57
generativity, 150
group work, 102–103, 106–107. *See also*
　　collaborative learning

holistic education, 151–152
Hollowell, Ed, 124–125
honesty, 139–140
hope, 158, 159
humanity, showing and encouraging,
　　88–92
humor, 72, 91–92

individual factors in learning, 53–54
information technology (IT) applications,
　　113–115, 119, 128. *See also*
　　technology
　　　　bringing the best thinking to a

discussion of, 153–155
communication and interactions,
　　117
and future of community colleges,
　　12
increasing array of, 9–11
presentation, 116–117
research and reference, 117–118
student application
　　and production, 115
student-driven learning, 115–116
institutional accountability, increasing
　　demands for, 8–9
institutional effectiveness, centrality of
　　learning and, 97–98
integrated perception, 82
intellectual skills, 54–56, 102
Internet, 122, 123, 153
interpersonal skills, 56–57
　　concern, 55
　　establishing rapport, 54

Johnson, S. I., 8

Klemp, G. O., Jr., 54–55

learner-centered psychological principles,
　　51–55
learning
　　is occurring all the time, 110
　　joy of, 83–84
　　love of, 27
learning-centered theory, 41, 46–47
learning colleges, v, 103
　　characteristics, 119
learning communities. *See* collaborative
　　learning
learning paradigm, 103
learning principles, comparative typology
　　of, 50–55
learning theory(ies), 44–46
　　applying, 50–51
　　linked to teaching practices, 49

lecture, 40–41
Limerick, Patricia, 40
listening to students, 90–91.
　　See also empathy
Lowman, J., 54

Marsh, H. W., 101
McKeachie, W. J., 38–39, 46, 47
Menges, R. J., 155–156
mentor, finding a, 135–136
meta-analysis, 48
Midlands Technical College (MTC), 98–99
motivation, intrinsic, 50
motivational factors in learning, 52–53, 102
motivational skills, 55, 57, 83–84, 87–88,
　　102

Nation at Risk, A, 37
National Institute for Staff and Organizational
　　Development (NISOD), vii, 3
　　　　conferences, 3, 25, 33
　　　　Teaching Excellence Award, vii,
　　　　　3–4, 17, 18
　　　　　recognition ceremonies, 3–4
nonverbal feedback, 106

O'Banion, T., 119
openness, 139–140
organization, 65–67

peer evaluation, 102
peer learning. *See* collaborative learning
people, love of, 27–28
perception, integrated, 82
policymakers, and purposes of education, 5
portfolios, 102
"practical magic," 133, 149
praise, 92–93
process-product research, 47
prototypes, 17–18
Pygmalion effect, 86
qualitative analysis, 48

redirection, 74
reflective practice, 48
research, 117–118
　　conducting classroom, 76–77
research design, advances in, 47–48
resources for services and programs,
　　declining, 9
respect, showing, 81–83
rewarding excellence, 92–93, 156–157
Richland College, 150
risk factors for students, 7
role models
　　negative, 32–33
　　positive, 30–32, 87
Roueche, John E., 4, 7, 8, 55–57, 99–100
Roueche, Suanne D., 7, 8, 151

Schneier, Bruce, 155
Schoch, R., 146
scholarship, new definitions of, 49–50
self-evaluation, 100
Senge, Peter, 40
Seymour, D., 157–158
small group instructional diagnosis (SGID),
　　102–103
social factors in learning, 53
student-centered learning theory, 46
student-teacher evaluations, 101–102
　　myths regarding, 101–102
students. *See also specific topics*
　　and purposes of education, 5
subject matter. *See also* teaching, of content
　　knowing, 61–63
　　love of, 27
survey method, quantitative, 20–22
Svinicki, M. D., 50–54
systematic practice, 48

Tagg, J., 46
"teachable moment," 81
teacher, reasons for becoming a
　　desire to make a difference, 25–26
　　love of one's life, 27–29
　　negative role models, 32–33

personal benefits, **29**
role models, family, friends, and
 significant others, **30–32**
serendipity, **29–30**
teachers, advice for beginning, **133,**
 145–146
 be flexible, **143**
 be open and honest, **139–140**
 be positive, **136–138**
 embrace notion of teaching life, **142**
 find mentor, **135–136**
 focus on students, **133–134**
 get involved in college activities, **145**
 make effort to be effective, **134–135**
 orient yourself to community college
  context and your college, **144–145**
 set high standards, **138–139**
 strive for balance, **142–143**
 use range of teaching techniques,
  140–142
 value student contributions, **143**
 value the intrinsic rewards, **143–144**
teaching of content, strategies for effective,
 61, 77. *See also* subject matter
  actively involving students, **69–70**
  affirming and redirecting, **74**
  being organized, **65–67**
  being student centered, **71–72**
  classroom research, **76–77**
  communicating clearly, **72–73**
  emphasizing relevance, application,
   and utility, **63–65**
  group work and collaborative
   learning, **73–74**
  humor, **72**
  knowing the subject, **61–63**
  setting high expectations and giving
   challenging work, **67–68**
  striving to foster high-level learning,
   68–69
  technology, **74–75**
  testing and assessment, **75–76**
  using a variety of methods, **70–71**
  visuals and learning resources, **75**
 love of, **28–29**
 methods of evaluating, **100, 108–110.**

See also assessing learning
  evaluations by peers, administrators,
   and external judges, **102**
  evaluations by students, **101–102**
  holistic evaluations, **102–103**
  self-evaluation, **100**
  student outcomes, **103**
 nobility of, **158**
 valuing the intrinsic rewards of,
  143–144
teaching effectively, **38–39.** *See also*
 specific topics
 clarity of instruction, **102**
 strategies for encouraging humor and
  humanity, **91–92**
  enthusiasm and sharing joy,
   83–84
  flexibility, **92**
  fostering motivation and success
   skills, **87–88**
  high expectations, **86–87**
  listening to students, **90–91**
  making contact, **88–90**
  praise, celebration, and reward,
   92–93
  showing care and empathy, **84–86**
  showing respect, **81–83**
  walking one's talk, **87**
teaching excellence, **38**
 historical landmarks and hallmarks,
  37–38
 implications for planning and practicing,
  149–159
  celebrate power of making a
   difference, **149–151**
  recognizing and rewarding
   excellence, **156–157**
  support interest in scholarship of
   teaching and learning, **151–153**
Teaching Excellence Award, **vii, 3–4,**
 17, 18
teaching methods, college
  exploring and using a range of,
   140–142
  successful, **39–43**
teaching practice(s), comparative typology

    of good, 55–57
technology. *See also* information technology
    (IT) applications
        as basic, necessary skill, **120**
        community as key issue in,
            124–128
        expense, **125**
        facilitates different kinds of
        learning, **122**
        gives students control over
        learning, **123**
        learning as key issue in, **119–124**
        making teaching more engaging,
            121–122
        need to keep human touch,
            127–128
        problems caused by fear, resistance,
            and true believers, **126–127**
        hardware and software, **126**
    unequal access to, **125–126**
    use of, requires time and training, **121**
    used by students for the novelty,
        123–124
testing, 75–76, **104**

University of Texas (UT) Teaching
    Excellence Award, **3**
Upcraft, M. L., **149–150**

Vaughan, G. B., **50**
visuals, **75**

Weinstein, Claire, **63**

Zwerling, L. S., **158–159**